LIFESAVERS

Tips for Success and Sanity
for Early Childhood Managers

Sue Baldwin

Insights Training & Consulting
Stillwater, Minnesota

Published by:
Insights Training & Consulting
818 West Maple Street
Stillwater, MN 55082

Edited by Mary Steiner Whelan
Book design by Ronna Hammer
Illustrated by Holly Welsh
Layout and production by Peregrine Graphics Services

Library of Congress Cataloging-in-Publication-Data

Baldwin, Sue
    Lifesavers: tips for sucess & sanity for early childhood
managers / Sue Baldwin.
        p.   cm.
    ISBN 0-9654439-0-6
    1. Child care services—United States—Administration. 2. Day care cen-
ters—United States—Administration. 3. Child care workers—job stress —
United States. 4. Communication in management—United States. I. Title.
HQ778.63.B35   1996
362.7'12'068—dc20   96-35829
                                                        CIP

Dedication

This book is dedicated to my grandson,
Nicholas Timothy Scheel,
who has provided me with the opportunity
to become a part time child care provider and
to experience the joy that being
a grandparent brings.

Acknowledgements

Many people were with me as I completed my book. I would like to thank them for throwing me a lifesaver when I needed help:

My family—Kris, Carrie, Tim, and Nick, for being who they are.

Vicki Bliss, whose friendship and humor helped keep me balanced throughout this endeavor.

Adam Bliss, my godson, who guided and helped me with my technology anxiety.

Mary Steiner Whelan, who offered me support and encouragement throughout this entire process, editing my words of wisdom. *For the Love of Children*, the successful book that Mary and her mother, Jean Steiner, wrote inspired me to write a book specifically for the child care professional.

Ronna Hammer, who helped coordinate all the behind-the-scenes events related to designing and self-publishing this book.

Child care professionals throughout the country who have inspired me with their dedication and commitment to making the world a better place for children and their families.

Table of Contents

Preface

After reading my first book, *The Early Childhood Super Director,* people commented that it sounded just like me. As you read *Lifesavers,* I hope you'll hear me speaking to you with humor and encouragement.

In early childhood, a wealth of material exists, designed to help child care professionals work with children. But few books assist directors and managers in their work with other adults. I wrote this book to help fill the void—to give you ideas you can use to reach the balance and excellence you work to achieve.

I hope you appreciate my humor and informal style—two ingredients, by the way, of successful interpersonal relationships. The book is designed to be picked up and read little-by-little, rather than cover-to-cover; because I know that, as child care professionals, you need something quick and informative. *Lifesavers* will provide you with practical information you can implement immediately on your job. I commend all child care professionals who are trying, in their own ways, to make this world a safer and better place for children.

Introduction

Since 1967, I have been teaching swimming activities for infants and preschoolers. I want young children to learn safety skills in the water. Sometimes that means learning how to use a lifesaver. I enjoy, and have a passion for, teaching young children swimming.

Since 1977, I've also been teaching adults who work in child care. They frequently tell me I teach them how to use lifesavers, too. The look of delight and relief on the faces of managers, when they really understand that they can have a great staff, a terrific program, and a life, isn't much different than the look on the faces of two year olds who jump into the water alone for the first time, and swim back to the side of the pool—secure in knowing they can grab a lifesaver if they need to.

So I offer this book of lifesavers to all professionals who sail the sometimes rough waters of child care and education—people who manage programs in centers, homes, preschools, on government bases, in school-age facilities, parenting programs, co-ops, Head Starts, and schools—people who dedicate themselves to making child care and education the best it can be.

If your title is manager, supervisor, director, principal, coordinator, lead teacher, or any other of the many titles of those who deal with the people who care for children, this book is for you. It will be a lifesaver in your daily interactions with parents, staff, government regulators, the community, and yourself. On its pages, you'll find hundreds of tips for success and sanity that really work.

You won't find a lot of research, statistics, or technical information, but rather, the nuts and bolts of what helps us maintain, and often excel, in the child care field. Much of the information is based on input from hundreds of managers I talked to as I traveled around the country doing workshops, retreats, and consultations.

The more training I do with child care professionals, the more I am convinced that working with children is the fun and rewarding aspect of this field. Interacting with adults is another matter, and often we are not specifically trained to do it well.

Everyone who works in the child care field knows how intense many situations can be, such as child abuse and neglect; parents who don't understand why their child is still in diapers at age two; children with special needs; and the government regulatory agencies who never cease to throw road blocks in our way. *Lifesavers* helps balance that stress with a touch of humor and effective techniques for dealing with other adults, as we try to maintain our sense of sanity.

I am a child care advocate. I am also an advocate for all managers who are responsible for producing a safe and appropriate environment for the children, *and* the adults who work in child care. I hope you enjoy *Lifesavers*. I am genuinely interested in hearing your comments and feedback. You may contact me at:

Sue Baldwin
818 West Maple Street
Stillwater, Minnesota 55082

I'd like to share with you this inspirational quote that someone shared with me, as I wish you strong breezes, and safe waters:

"A hundred years from now it will not matter what my bank account was, the sort of house I lived in, or the kind of car I drove–but the world may be different, because I was important in the life of a child."
                                                            – Anonymous

---

Happy career sailing, and remember to grab a lifesaver when you need a little extra support.

—Sue Baldwin

Self-Care for the Caregiver

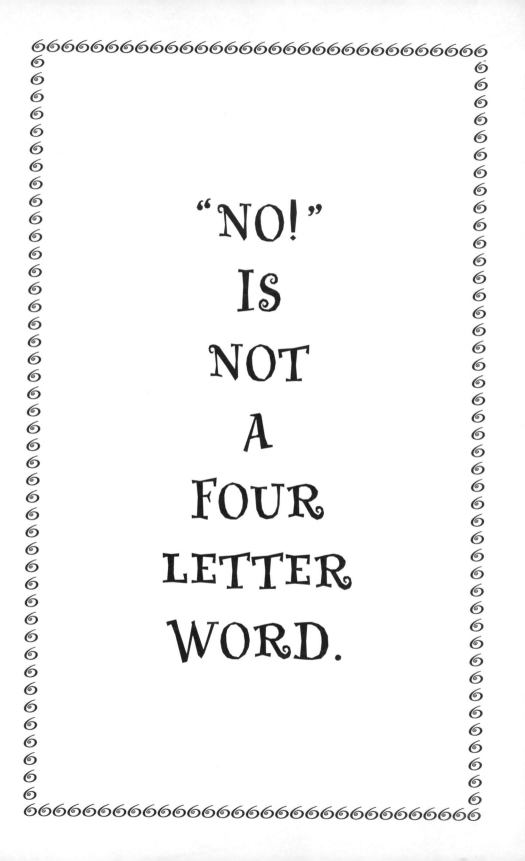

Self Quiz

Child care professionals are very good at caring for others, but often lack self-care skills. Sometimes they fear feeling guilty or selfish. Check yes or no after each statement to determine your level of wellness.

	YES	NO
1. My relationships are more giving than getting.	___	___
2. I feel drained at the end of the week from taking care of others.	___	___
3. I resent others who seem to have more energy than I do.	___	___
4. I have difficulty letting others know what I need.	___	___
5. I have trouble trusting what others say to me.	___	___
6. I find myself working more and playing less.	___	___
7. I'm experiencing more demands than rewards in my personal and professional life.	___	___
8. I don't get an adequate amount of sleep each night.	___	___
9. I know that I should cut down on the amount of sugar and caffeine I consume.	___	___
10. I sometimes use alcohol to feel better.	___	___
11. I rarely exercise three or more times a week.	___	___
Total	___	___

If you checked yes on more than four of the above statements, I would strongly suggest that you take some time for yourself. In any case, read the following chapters. You will learn something that will help you take better care of the important person you are.

Survival Tips

1. Develop and maintain a group of friends in both your personal and professional lives who can offer you support.

2. Develop a smaller group of friends with whom you can maintain trusting relationships. Ask those people to be honest with you and return the honesty to them.

3. Let others know what you need from them. People can't read your mind to know what you need.

4. Evaluate your support system to see who is giving support to you and who is getting support from you.

5. Ask for venting time with peer professionals as well as personal friends.

6. Don't give advice to others unless they ask for it. Even when they ask, be cautious about giving advice.

7. Encourage yourself and others to find your/their own solutions to problems. Brainstorming ideas is an alternative to giving direct advice.

8. Get enough sleep each night. Don't wait for the weekend to do a crash course in resting and sleeping.

9. Watch for signs of sleep depravation such as touching your eyelids or feeling the way you did after your seventh-grade slumber party.

10. Learn what can happen to your body and mental state when you consume too much caffeine, sugar, and/or alcohol.

11. Reclaim your time and energy for exercise. Develop a plan that really works for you.

12. Learn and practice saying "No" techniques with others in your personal and professional lives.

Sue's Solutions

What Really Works

6   As child care professionals we learn to take care of others. Caring for other people seems to be easier for us than taking care of ourselves. Before it gets too late, health and age wise, we need to let go of the guilt that we often associate with self-care. Guilt is an emotion that gets a lot of attention and uses up tons of energy. It is also an emotion that we can put into perspective.

6   Because managing a child care program is filled with interpersonal relationships all day, finding time to be alone in your personal life is important. Just as we all need people in our lives, we also need time to ourselves—time to reflect on our personal values and goals—and time to just vegetate.

6   Block out time for recreation and leisure. If you don't place a high value on these activities, they will be among the first to go when you have a crisis to manage. Child care managers are good at working intently all day, but often forget to schedule time to play. You can choose from a variety of active forms of recreation (walking, biking, skiing) to more sedentary activities (reading, going to movies or concerts, or working in the garden).

6   An old proverb says "Death is Nature's Way of Slowing Us Down." You can (although you may not believe it) slow down without dying. Alone time, recreation, and leisure events are all ways of breaking out of the fast lane in which we sometimes feel trapped. At times, all we may be able to do is say to ourselves, "Keep breathing." Deep breaths are an easy way of slowing down for a little while.

6   I've devoted a whole chapter in this book to looking at humor in our lives, because humor is an essential element of self-care. We need to be able to laugh at ourselves and to find humor wherever we can.

❻ I would recommend that you do this excercise whenever you are feeling drained and empty. It's simple to reproduce, and will probably change often.

   a. Make a circle and put your first name in the middle.

   b. Write the first names of people with whom you have regular contact around the outside of the circle.

   c. Draw a line from each of their names to your name. The circle will look like a wagon wheel with spokes.

   d. Make each line into an arrow. Here are your choices for the arrows:

       ◄——— if you are giving more support to the other person;

       ———► if you are getting more support from the other person;

       ◄——► if you are getting and giving mutually to each other.

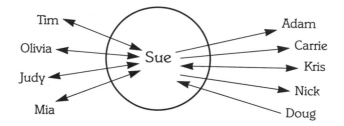

   e. Total up the number of arrows for each of the three types.

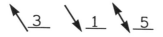

The arrows will validate how you are feeling in your relationships. When I do this exercise in training sessions, people sometimes ask if they can add their pets. Since my dogs are very important in my life, the answer is "yes." For example, during the times when K.C., my cocker spaniel, causes problems with neighbors and the local police, the arrow is definitely going OUT.

❻ Child care professionals tend to use too much caffeine and sugar, perhaps because of their daily frantic pace. I would urge you to look at how caffeine and sugar are affecting your well-being. A woman in one of my classes told us about her visit to a doctor when she was 24 years old. She had found a lump in her breast, which surgeons removed and found to be benign.

After quizzing her about her health and eating habits, her doctor told her to immediately discontinue using any products that contain caffeine. Ten years had passed since her surgery when she related her experience to the class. She told how scared she was then, and how much better she's felt since following her doctor's advice.

Be aware that sugar gives you the instant boost that you think you need to keep going in the middle of the afternoon, but remember, after every boost a bigger slump occurs.

6 Alcohol also causes boosts and slumps in your emotional well-being, similar to those changes sugar causes. Although research shows that people who aren't addicted to alcohol can safely consume a small amount, monitor your usage.

A question that you can ask yourself about your consumption of alcohol is "Am I drinking to avoid addressing certain problems or to make myself feel better?" A lot of information about alcohol abuse is available from many health-care-oriented sources, should you choose to learn more about this topic.

6 Adequate sleep and rest requirements can be different for every person reading this book. My older daughter used to need at least ten hours of sleep each night. Then, she became a mom. It's been quite a while since she's gotten through the night without her son awakening her. But her body has learned to adjust. She has also learned how to take naps whenever the opportunity arises.

If you are feeling irrational, irritable, are more susceptible to illness, and unable to operate at an optimum level, you might want to look at your sleep patterns. Don't count on the weekends for catching up. Rather, make a conscientious effort to get the sleep you need on a daily basis.

6 The kind of physical exercise that is healthy varies from person to person. Research documents that exercise is a stress reducer, and done on a regular basis, it also contributes to a healthy body. I find it easier to get into a routine if I have someone else who will exercise with me. "Misery loves company," as you know.

For several years, I met another child care professional at a local YWCA, and we walked and swam laps two to three mornings a week before going into work. Walking is something almost everyone can do, and it doesn't require washing the chlorine off your body or out of your hair.

You can meet a friend to walk with in the middle of the day, when you feel like you need a time out. Whatever exercise you choose, just do it!

6 People who work in child care settings tend to be more susceptible to contagious diseases because they are around young children and their germs. One of the dubious fringe benefits of our jobs is the building up of our immune systems.

Taking off work when one is sick can create a dilemma. Because people who work in group settings deal with a shortage of substitutes, the question is, "Do I work when I'm sick?" If we are focusing on self-care, we need to take care of ourselves when we are mentally or physically ill.

Set a high priority for developing substitute lists, and role model for others what they need to do when they find themselves too sick to work with children.

Many people today are simplifying their lives. I'm strongly in favor of this trend, which can encompass many areas of our lives: the transportation we use; the houses we live in; the number of material possessions we own; how much energy we consume; and the amount of clutter that surrounds us.

Some cultures and religions adopt simplicity as a way of life. We can think about this concept in terms of self-care. If we personalize the idea of simplicity, we can make some specific changes to use less and enjoy more. Some examples are:

- If the television breaks, don't fix it.

- Watch a leaf fall all the way from a tall tree to the ground.

- Learn to play a musical instrument.

- Walk or bike places rather than driving a motor vehicle.

- Spend thirty minutes at a beach, lake, or other body of water, and listen to the stillness.

• Write a letter, using a favorite pen rather than a computer

A simpler life is often a healthier one.

☺ Wouldn't it be wonderful if others could guess what we need without us verbalizing our needs and desires? I really don't think anything will make this fantasy come true in our lifetimes—we need to begin to face reality.

Friends, relatives, and co-workers can't read our minds, so we have to take a risk and ask for what we need. Sometimes, maybe even more than once in a while, I have been known to get a stubborn streak and defiantly say, "Fine, I'll just do it myself." I've actually gotten mad at other people, because they couldn't figure out what I needed without me telling them. Does this sound familiar? Asking for help from others means that we are human and vulnerable.

We are risking rejection when we ask for help but without asking, we keep ourselves isolated and detached from others. Take a chance. Ask someone for help. Burn your Super Person cape, and join the human race.

☺ Wellness is something we forget to emphasize. As managers, we are role models. When we set wellness as a priority, others will notice and perhaps begin to evaluate their own personal lifestyles.

Ask Yourself These Questions

Do I consider my health a matter of chance or something in my control?
If you don't take control of your self-care, you, no one else, will have to suffer the consequences. Perhaps you know a person who has become very ill and is full of regret for not having been proactive about self-care. You don't want to let that happen to you.

It's not too late. People who have been diagnosed with life-threatening illness have made dramatic lifestyle changes and improved their quality of life.

How can I slow down in my daily living?

I truly believe if we don't slow ourselves down, an outside force (you can decide what to call that force) will help us do so. I've received numerous warnings that I have to slow down my lifestyle, among them, illness, a serious traffic accident, and a dangerous skid on an icy road. Make a commitment to yourself, and to someone else, about the changes you are going to enact immediately.

How can I change life-long habits such as smoking or eating too much sugar?

Many self-help groups throughout the country can help you make changes with chemicals that are addictive. Your doctor and supportive friends/relatives are other people whom you can turn to for assistance. Give yourself permission to ask for help.

How can I practice saying "Yes" to myself?

The "Yes" response always seems to pop out of our mouths when other people request something. Then, we have another burden or obligation to fulfill. Maybe we just want to be liked or needed. Maybe we are flattered that people ask us to do things. Maybe we feel important or powerful when people need us. Learn that "No" is a word you can learn to use regularly. Try these specific techniques:

STALL. We think that we have to give an answer right away. That's not usually true. Practice saying, "Let me think about that and get back to you."

EVALUATE. How much time is this person asking of you, and do you want to make this commitment? Ask exactly what you will be expected to do. Then, decide if you have the time or the desire.

ELIMINATE GUILT. Feeling guilty is a waste of time and energy unless you have committed a crime or violated ethical standards. Saying "Yes" because of guilt is not a healthy response.

BE SELECTIVE. Don't get carried away with the flattery of being asked to do something. If it's a social event make sure it's something you want to attend before you decide to say "Yes, I'd love to."

PRIORITIZE. Make your own plans a top priority before taking care of everyone else who makes demands on you. "I'm already overcommitted," is a response that can be brief and true when delivered to a person making the request for your time.

Summary

Self-care is difficult to maintain, because we're doing something that we weren't trained to do. As child care professionals, we were taught how to take care of other people. Now the focus is on ourselves.

We can use our connection with children to teach them how to care for themselves. Wouldn't it be wonderful if today's children learned self-care, so, when they are adults, they won't have to struggle with this issue as most of us do?

Be open with children, parents, and co-workers about what your plan is for self-care. Others may get excited with you about a new endeavor, and want to join you on your road to wellness.

Take a few minutes to complete the following personal contract for change. Be sure to sign and date the contract as you make the commitment to yourself.

Personal Contract For Change

After reading this chapter on self-care, I am going to make the following changes:

In my recreation and leisure time I am going to:

    A.

    B.

    C.

I'm going to look at my relationships and make these changes:

    PERSON   CHANGE

    A.   A.

    B.   B.

    C.   C.

I'm going to work less and play more by:

    A.

    B.

    C.

This is how I'm going to say "No" to someone else and "Yes" to myself:

    A.

    B.

    C.

_____   _____
        signed   date

Too Much to Do
Too Little Time

BE PROACTIVE. THE TIME TO LEARN HOW TO SWIM IS NOT WHEN YOU ARE DROWNING.

Survival Quiz

Do you ever feel like the mad hatter in *Alice in Wonderland?* Try to slow down long enough to take this short quiz on how you spend your time. Check yes or no next to the following statements and total your score:

	YES	NO
1. I feel as though I'm constantly racing from one activity to another.	___	___
2. I have a hard time focusing on one thing at a time.	___	___
3. I have been labeled a procrastinator by some friends and family.	___	___
4. I wish there were more than 24 hours in a day so I could get more done.	___	___
5. Sometimes I feel as though I'm managing crises rather than a program.	___	___
6. I have a hard time staying in the present without thinking of other things and/or people I should be taking care of.	___	___
7. I overcommit myself by biting off more than I can chew.	___	___
8. I have a difficult time prioritizing, because everything seems important.	___	___
9. My friends have suggested that I slow down, but I don't have the time.	___	___
10. Things just never seem to move fast enough or get done fast enough for me.	___	___
Total	___	___

If you checked yes on three or more of the above statements, I suggest that you find a nice quiet place to relax and read the rest of this chapter.

Survival Tips

1. Get organized. You will feel more in control and will be better at carrying out your responsibilities.

2. Carry a planner with you that has all your vital information.

3. Make a daily list of things and people who need your attention. Take the two least important things off the list.

4. Break tasks down into bite-sized chunks.

5. Schedule your work day, allowing for interruptions, unscheduled events, and problems.

6. Don't plan out every minute of the day. Allow for spontaneous activities.

7. Leave time open on the weekend for yourself, friends, and family.

8. Make procrastination a thing of the past. Do it right away!

9. Use timesaving techniques such as answering machines. Write notes to people who want more of your time than you can give, and use FAX machines when you need to send or receive something fast.

10. Eliminate interruptions that can derail you from meeting a deadline. Put others in charge so you can do work that requires concentration.

11. Turn meetings into time well-spent. Don't create or participate in unnecessary meetings.

12. Bring busy work to do when you're waiting for appointments at the doctor's or dentist's, or at the garage while the mechanic repairs your car. Or, use the time for much needed relaxing. Don't use it for worrying.

13. Offer praise to yourself for all you've accomplished.

Sue's Solutions

What Really Works

I was almost finished with this book when someone who knows me well asked me if I talked about my father when I discussed making lists. I couldn't believe that I forgot about Phil Lyman's famous lists on yellow paper. Lists were an integral part of my family's life. My father *always* had his yellow lists in the breast pocket of his shirt. The lists would be with him wherever he went: to the office, to do yard work, and even when we went on vacations. Every morning at the breakfast table, my father would review with my mother what tasks she was to do for the day. He lived by and for his yellow paper lists. Though several years have gone by since his death, our family still smiles about how his lists, even when he was in the hospital, remained a part of who he was.

6 List-making is controversial. Some people report that the habit helps them get and stay organized. Others say, when they see everything they have to do, they feel overwhelmed. Here are some tips for people who want to use the list-making technique:

- Use one list. Keep it in the same place, in plain view, rather than in a desk drawer, so you can see it and be aware of what you need to accomplish.

- Have a separate page for each day with subtitles: "Phone Calls," "Errands," "Meetings," and other must-do items.

- Mark off your accomplishments, and move things you didn't get done to the next day.

- Review and reprioritize your list every day.

- At the end of the week evaluate the tasks that you moved to the following day because they didn't get done. Are they important?

- Don't rely on your memory. Write tasks down as soon as you think of them, so you can clear your head for more important thoughts.

- Set deadlines for your projects. Let others in your program know what the deadlines are for certain projects, such as filing reports for licensing.

☉ Restrict the number of calendars you are using. This is important. At one point I had five calendars: a desk and wall calendar at work; a daily planner that I carried with me; and calendars by the telephones both upstairs and downstairs at home.

No wonder I felt stressed. I had to keep remembering to write events down in five different places. A daily planner that you carry with you should be your master calendar, coordinating both personal and professional events.

☉ A common mistake people who want to be organized make, is to schedule their time so tightly with structured events that they don't have time for unplanned, spontaneous activities. Allow time for interruptions and crises that might occur.

☉ Make time to be alone a priority in your personal and professional lives. When we get scattered moving from one event to another, it's hard to make time for ourselves. No one will do it for you. Creating and spending time with yourself will help you feel less resentful toward others when they make demands of you.

☉ Lists help you avoid procrastination, which is a time waster that's easily cured. People don't admit they're procrastinating. They say they get busy with other, more important things. Procrastination can become more than a habit. It can become a way of life. Do you fall into any of these categories of procrastinators?

- *Crisis makers* who tend to get very involved with different projects. Their lives seem to be full of people and problems who constantly need them—right now!

- *Worriers* who have difficulty making decisions and tend to get paralyzed when starting a new project, because they doubt their ability. They need approval and assistance from others before starting.

- *Perfectionists* who want things done their way and have difficulty delegating tasks. They may become preoccupied with details and have very high, often unreachable standards for themselves and others.

- *Overdoers* who run around doing lots of things and taking care of a lot of people, but don't accomplish much. They are the people who complain about having too much to do and too little time. They often get involved in other people's problems at the expense of solving their own.

- *Dreamers* who wait for opportunities to present themselves without digging in and doing the job. They have great ideas about what they would like to do, but seldom put their ideas into action.

6 Now that we have identified some of the people who might have problems with procrastination, let's look at specific tips for dealing with the problem:

- Make and keep deadlines.

- Delegate tasks to others. If you can't delegate it, and you don't have time to do it, dump it.

- Tell others what you plan to do. When we make others aware of our intentions, it sometimes helps us make a personal commitment.

- Don't start what you can't finish, and finish what you start.

- Minimize your distractions: phone calls, snacking, and chatting with others.

- Get organized. This applies to both your home and your work environment.

- Just get started. Sometimes getting started is the biggest obstacle to overcome.

- Remember you don't have to be perfect.

- Commit to spending 30 minutes on a particular project and stick to that commitment without allowing for distractions.

6 As I wrote this book, I could see how powerful distractions are. The phone rings, the dogs need to go outside, and someone stops by unexpectedly. People won't help you reduce distractions. You need to set some boundaries.

A good time to do work that requires concentration is when distractions are at a minimum. Early in the morning before staff and parents are calling in, or late in the afternoon, when other professionals are there to take care of the needs of children and other adults, are times you might want to block off for undisturbed work.

6 Meetings can either be very effective or time-wasters. Don't schedule or participate in meetings just for the sake of getting people together. Staff meetings should be part of every child care program, but make sure they are effective with the following tips:

- Have a starting and ending time that you and others adhere to.

- Post the agenda. Ask others to read it before the meeting so they can participate more effectively.

- Time the agenda so people will know how much time will be available for discussion.

- Have a timekeeper whose responsibility is to keep the meeting on task.

- Don't get sidetracked with items that are not on the agenda, and discourage others from doing so.

- Delegate taking the minutes to someone other than the timekeeper or the person who is conducting the meeting.

- If an agenda item requires discussion, plan in the necessary time before the meeting begins.

- Don't have too many items on the agenda for the amount of time scheduled.

Schedule meetings so there are minimal, if any, distractions and interruptions. Many programs encourage staff to attend meetings by holding them immediately after work, preceding them with a meal, and following them with a brief in-service training session. (The Federal Department of Labor requires that all staff are paid to attend staff meetings.)

6 Remember to take busy work with you for time between appointments, as I suggested earlier. I bring my personal check book to balance, a copy of *Child Care Information Exchange*, and bills to pay. This technique is effective for making the most of idle time.

6 Technology is providing us with many timesaving machines:

- *FAX machines* allow you to send pieces of correspondence out immediately, and they're affordable.

- *Answering machines* permit you to work without interruptions and also to send messages to another person without spending time repeating your efforts.

- *Paging systems* make parents more accessible for sick or injured children.

- *Cellular phones* are useful on field trips and playgrounds to give staff instant access to assistance in time of trouble.

The material in this chapter augments what you'll find in Chapter 4, "What is This Mess Called Stress?" and Chapter 11, "Delegating is More Than Just Dumping." Effective managers make time management a priority in their personal and professional lives.

Ask Yourself These Questions

Should I make a routine of doing more than one thing at a time?

Sometimes it's productive and efficient to do more than one thing at a time. When you're on hold on the telephone, or sitting in a waiting room, are appropriate times to get work done. Driving a car, or having a conversation with another person, are not times when doing two things simultaneously is effective.

Why do I have a hard time finishing reports at night?
Each of us has an internal clock which makes us more effective in the morning or at night. Some people love to get up early and get a quick start on the day. Others do their best work and play after dinner. Decide whether you're a morning or a night person. I know that I do best in the early morning hours. So, I don't wait to do reports or budget planning at night.

How can I allow time for myself without feeling guilty or selfish?
Recognize that you are more effective, with and for others, when you allow time for yourself. Resentment builds up in us when we continually take care of everything and everyone else before ourselves. Ask people you trust to help support you with the task of finding time for yourself.

Summary

Child care managers report that their jobs are *never* dull and boring. In fact, some say they wish there were more than 24 hours a day to get their jobs done. We begin our days full of great intentions about what needs to happen during the day; and then, we often shift into crisis management: unplugging toilets, filling in in the classroom for a sick teacher, helping out with disruptive children, and tracking down parents to pick up their sick child.

Learning to organize and prioritize are essential for effective management. If these are skills you know you need to improve on, finish this chapter and then do some further work on the topic. Go to the library and find a book on time management, take a class on the subject; or ask others how they manage their jobs with so much to do in so little time. Just do it!

Personal Contract For Change

I will take the time, right now, to make changes in how I manage my time.

I am going to stop procrastinating in the following ways:

How I Procrastinate	Changes I Will Make
A.	A.
B.	B.
C.	C.

These are my short-term professional goals and time projection:

Goal	By When
A.	A.
B.	B.
C.	C.

Steps related to time management that I will make for more effective meetings:

A.

B.

C.

D.

_____   _____
            signed   date

Balancing Our Personal And Professional Lives

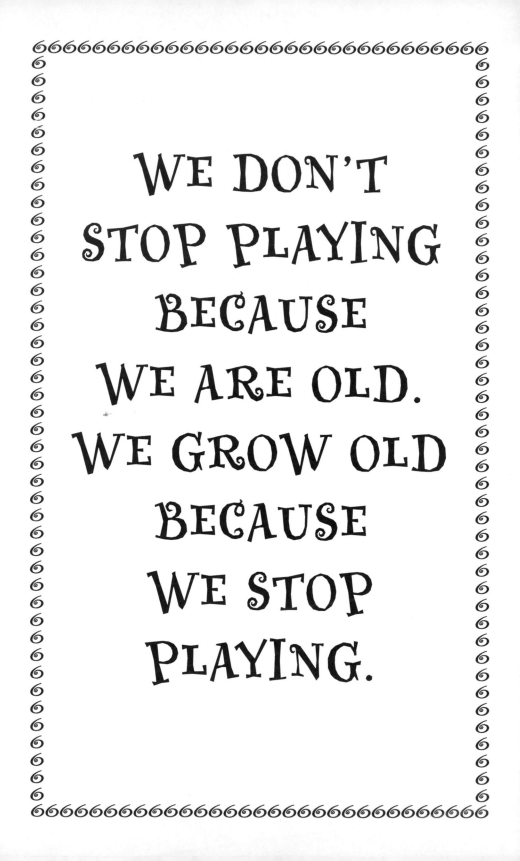

WE DON'T
STOP PLAYING
BECAUSE
WE ARE OLD.
WE GROW OLD
BECAUSE
WE STOP
PLAYING.

Self Quiz

Take a few minutes to assess the balance you have now between your personal and professional lives. Answer each statement with either yes or no. You'll note that "sometimes" is not a choice. If in doubt, check yes if you do something more than 50% of the time.

	YES	NO
1. I find myself working more hours now than I did six months ago.	___	___
2. I have less time to spend with friends and relatives.	___	___
3. When people talk to me, I feel scattered and have a hard time listening.	___	___
4. I feel more serious and less playful than I have in the past.	___	___
5. I don't have time to exercise on a regular basis.	___	___
6. I take work home in the evening because I don't have enough time during the day.	___	___
7. I admire people who have careers where they can separate their personal and professional lives.	___	___
8. I don't have enough time to get the support I need from other professionals in the child care field.	___	___
9. At times I wish I was working strictly with children and not in a supervisory role.	___	___
10. It seems as though I am giving lots more support to others than I'm receiving for myself.	___	___
Total	___	___

If you checked yes on three or more statements, you are on a tight rope and need to develop a safety net. Keep reading this chapter for suggestions that will help you get your personal and professional lives in balance.

Survival Tips

1. Have people in your life who have interests other than child care.

2. Set your own personal limitations with others. Let them know where your boundaries begin and end.

3. Invest yourself 100% while at work. Then, when it's time to leave, walk away and put your work behind you.

4. As you walk, bike, or drive home from work, start thinking about people and events in your personal life.

5. Take time to really be present with your friends and family. Keep your mind from wandering back to work by concentrating on listening and talking to others about other things that matter.

6. Become part of a professional support group. Get and give support to your peers.

7. Learn how to love to sweat. Develop an exercise program for yourself that includes both winding down and relaxing.

8. Prioritize what is *really* important for you to achieve in your personal and professional lives.

9. Add some spice and variety to your life. Don't get caught up in the "same old, same old." Hang out with people who can be silly, fun, and playful.

10. Sit down today and make a list of what you want to accomplish with your life.

11. Don't isolate yourself. Satisfy your basic need to belong, and become involved by joining activities or organizations that match your values and goals.

12. Protect your alone time. Stake out your time, and don't allow others to infringe on it.

13. Let others know what you need, and be willing to accept help when needed.

14. Maintain a balanced lifestyle, which includes paying attention to your physical, emotional, and spiritual needs.

Sue's Solutions

What Really Works

When I felt like I was walking on a tight rope without a safety net, I made the following changes in my life:

6 I sat down with a pencil and paper and wrote down how much time I was spending at work and in my personal life. Writing the facts on paper kept me honest about how I used my time. It became clearer that I had to make changes. I was spending too much time at work and not enough time on my personal life.

6 I practiced what I preached. I immediately decided to make some changes. I must admit that people at work were not thrilled when I announced that I was limiting my time to a normal work week. However, I did get support from friends who could see how out of balance I was.

6 I found that one of my main problems was that I didn't have enough time for myself. All day at work, I answered people's needs; and when I got home, the people there needed me, too.

6 I created "Time for Me" which gave me permission to spend at least thirty minutes daily without any have to's. If I needed to nap or stare at a blank wall, that was okay.

   Warning: Remember, you'll need to become very protective of this time and honor the commitment you've made to yourself.

6 I decided that I needed to reinstate personal and professional limits with friends, family, and co-workers.

6 Since I didn't have a support network available at work, I created one. I called three other child care professionals from other local programs, and we started having dinner together once a week. We supported each other well, because we spoke the same language and shared the same problems.

6 I stopped taking work home, and I stopped taking my personal

problems to work. This was not easy to do. I found that I had to discipline myself and consciously decide to separate the two areas of my life.

6   I found another child care manager who wanted to start a personal-fitness program. We met three mornings a week before work and walked together. We benefited from the exercise, fresh air, and the time together.

6   I took a free nutrition class at the local hospital, which empha-sized easy-to-cook meals. I met people at these classes who wanted to focus on good health rather than the perils of child care. The information and people enhanced my balanced lifestyle.

6   I cut down on my daily caffeine and sugar intake and achieved a sense of internal calmness. I wasn't as jittery, and my emotions felt more balanced.

6   I figured out that we have four distinct components in our lives we need to address:

- Home: partner, children, pets, home maintenance

- Career: stress, child care, deadlines, and other responsibilities

- Recreation: sports, entertainment, and hobbies

- Community Involvement: church, community, school, and professional organizations

I had a lot of balls to juggle at one time. Just becoming aware of how much I was doing gave me permission to be more patient with myself. I developed a new sense of pride and accomplish-ment, and I really do get a lot done.

6   To create more balance in my personal life I came up with five areas that needed to be addressed weekly. This is what I did:

FAMILY TIME: Attended athletic activities with my children, planned time to do fun things with my family, realized that Saturday morning was for chores, and that Sunday was for spending quality time together.

RECREATION: Played racquetball with friends, walked with my exercise buddy, and began biking with another neighborhood family.

BUILDING RELATIONSHIPS: Volunteered at a local nursing home, invited a co-worker to dinner, built a relationship with my neighbor, and spent time alone with my significant other.

COMMUNICATING: Enrolled in a class at the local community college, went shopping with a friend and tried on ugly bathing suits during the middle of winter (lots of laughs!), and talked on the phone with another friend who had moved out of state.

TIME ALONE: Read a book, wrote in my journal, listened to a relaxation tape, and took a nap.

Where did I find the time to do all of this? By managing my time, prioritizing, and making changes. It's truly amazing how many hours we have in a week when we're not spending all of them at work.

Ask Yourself These Questions

At what cost am I willing to live an unbalanced life?
I know that when I work too much and play too little, it affects my mood and relationships. When my life is unbalanced, my stress level increases and puts me at risk for accidents. When I was trying to be Super Director and living my life in the fast lane, I had an automobile accident that put me in the hospital with a concussion.

A friend came to visit me and asked, "Should I act surprised to see you here?" She was aware of my fast pace and out-of-balance lifestyle, and she suggested that I consider this accident a warning to slow down.

How will I know if my life is becoming unbalanced?
Your close friends and relatives may be the first people to say something to you, because you give them clues. People whose lives are out of balance feel overwhelmed, irritable, short-tempered, and tired; and they seem to be always in a hurry.

If this description fits you, stop what you are doing. Don't be defensive about how you're spending your time; be honest with yourself. Are you working too much or giving too much of yourself to people who ask for your support?

How can I make some changes in how I spend my personal and professional time?

The first step is to see on paper how you spend your time. Complete the circles of life as illustrated. Look at an average week from last month. Use your personal and work calendars to help you remember. You'll note the circles represent REALITY and DREAMS. Your dream circle will show how you'll make changes to create a more balanced lifestyle.

My Examples

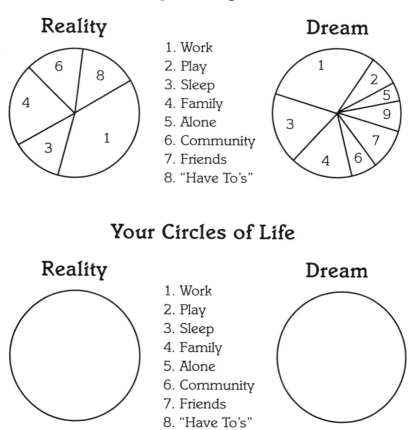

Reality

Dream

1. Work
2. Play
3. Sleep
4. Family
5. Alone
6. Community
7. Friends
8. "Have To's"

Your Circles of Life

Reality

Dream

1. Work
2. Play
3. Sleep
4. Family
5. Alone
6. Community
7. Friends
8. "Have To's"

Summary

I think most of us forget to consider one of the intangible fringe benefits that comes with our careers–the benefit of being surrounded by little people who are learning, playing, and growing every day.

As adults, we lose some of those childlike characteristics we see in young children. Children take risks. They laugh, play, are honest with others. They experience and express real feelings, and they slow down when their bodies tell them they're tired.

When we adults work on creating a balanced lifestyle, children can be our teachers. Pay attention to their childlike characteristics and balance those with our adult responsibilities. When we blend childlike and responsible characteristics together, we can have a career we enjoy; friends and family who appreciate each other; and a sense of self, which includes personal and professional goals and values; and a positive attitude.

Personal Contract For Change

After reading the information in the preceding chapter, I am going to make the following changes to help balance my personal and professional lives:

Things I Will Start Doing   Things I Will Stop Doing

    A.   A.

    B.   B.

    C.   C.

I will be more childlike in these ways:

    A.

    B.

    C.

I'm going to make these changes to become more internally balanced with my physical, emotional, and spiritual self:

    A.

    B.

    C.

I will seek these people out to gain support for myself during this time of change:

    A.

    B.

    C.

_____   _____

      signed   date

What Is
This Mess
Called Stress?

STRESS IS WHEN YOUR GUT SAYS "NO WAY!" AND YOUR MOUTH SAYS "SURE, I'D BE GLAD TO!"

Self Quiz

Reflect on your present personal and professional life, and answer each question. I know that you might be tempted to want to answer "sometimes," but that's too wishy-washy. Check yes or no and then total your score.

	YES	NO
1. Am I thinking/dreaming about my job at night when I should be sleeping?	___	___
2. Do my friends/relatives say that I seem more irritable and crabby than usual?	___	___
3. Have I forgotten the meaning of the word "fun"?	___	___
4. Am I experiencing physical symptoms of stress (tightness of shoulders, knot in my stomach, or headaches)?	___	___
5. Am I seeing close friends and relatives less frequently?	___	___
6. Am I working more and accomplishing less?	___	___
7. Do I tire more easily than I used to or do I feel more fatigued than energetic?	___	___
8. Am I more cynical and disenchanted in both my personal and professional lives?	___	___
9. Am I noticing a difference in my level of tolerance of others?	___	___
10. Do I feel that I have given 150% of myself to others and am exhausted at the end of the day?	___	___
Total	___	___

If you checked yes on three or more questions, continue reading this chapter. If you checked yes on all of the above questions, call your travel agent immediately; and book a vacation.

Survival Tips

Personal Life

1. Take a deep breath. Take three more deep breaths.

2. Close your eyes and picture yourself somewhere, safe and relaxed.

3. Develop a professional support network.

4. Go out for lunch with a friend, and don't talk about work.

5. Decide if this stress is time-limited and will be gone after the crisis you're experiencing.

6. Take action now and make positive changes. Don't be a victim.

7. Take a bubble bath.

8. Laugh out loud at a funny joke.

9. Take an aerobics class.

10. Go try on funny clothes with a friend.

11. Find releases for your feeling of stress: dance, listen to music, walk, swim, or plant a garden.

12. If shopping is your bag, go spend time at a mall.

13. If you hate shopping, and it causes you stress, stay away from the mall.

14. Buy a jar of bubbles, and do what your mother told you never to do: blow the bubbles inside the house, or keep them in your car, and blow them out your window when you're waiting in a traffic jam.

15. Make a To Do list of things you have already done.

16. Pop popcorn without a lid on the popper.

You can add to this list. I know you can find things you can do to prevent stress from taking over your life. During the check-in at a class I taught for child care coordinators, a woman shared that she had just been to a stress-management class. One of the tips she learned was to dance naked in front of her pet.

As she told this story, the entire class laughed aloud for five minutes. I'm sure each of us was visualizing what we would look like doing this silly exercise. When we finally calmed down, we started talking about how humor and laughter are stress releasers.

Do you know that a hundred laughs are equal, as a healthy exercise, to ten minutes of rowing? Think about it, you don't have to leave your house and go find a boat to row. You can just laugh. Laughter is free and fun.

Also, it can be contagious. Have you ever been in a serious meeting or in a quiet place when something you thought of brought a smile to your face? I have a very good friend I love to be with, because we appreciate each other's sense of humor and find silly things to laugh about. Maybe we are catching on to the healing power of laughter.

Have you noticed the rise in comedy clubs recently throughout the country? I just went to a movie where the entire audience roared with laughter at Robin Williams' comic routines. We need to laugh. We also need to become more gentle with ourselves.

Professional Life

Let's look at some practical ideas that you can incorporate into your program to reduce, not only your stress level, but also lessen the tension for your staff:

1. Have peaceful and relaxing music playing in your program.

2. Budget in money to hire a floater, someone who can fill in when staff are out sick or who can work in the program in various roles. You won't have to scramble to find last minute substitutes. When not subbing, the person can be that much-needed extra pair of hands.

3. Physically redesign your program to reduce stress. Have an area for parents to sign in/out. Place the cubbies so the children have their own space, and let in natural light wherever possible.

4. Develop a room for the staff to use during their breaks away from the children. Have resources related to stress reduction available for them in the room: adult stress toys, herbal tea, decaffeinated pop or juice, posters depicting nature scenes, and relaxation tapes for listening.

5. Encourage staff to share funny things they heard the children say, through the newsletter or the staff log book.

6. Teach the staff relaxation and stress reduction techniques they can use with the children. Children certainly feel stress, but can learn coping techniques at an early age that will be valuable for a lifetime.

7. Educate the staff, parents, and the children about food that is good for stress reduction. Suggest staying away from sugar and foods that are low in nutritional value.

8. Develop a stress barometer in your program and pay attention to possible signs of decreased levels of tolerance for stress. If your licenser is due for an on-site inspection, staff are out sick, and you have an irate parent coming for a conference; put your stress reduction plans into action immediately. If you're feeling stressed, your staff is probably feeling the same way.

9. Plan a staff retreat in the middle of winter. You can use this opportunity for a combination of in-service training and staff bonding time.

10. Don't forget how to play. You're working in an environment that encourages play for children, so use it to your advantage.

11. Stress can be very serious, and even deadly, if left untreated. In one of my classes, a participant told how dangerous her stress had been. She was the owner of a program, and she was experiencing physical and emotional signs of stress. When she consulted with her physician, she learned that she had an ulcer and early signs of heart damage.

    She sold her program. But, because she was committed to working with children, she took a job in another child care center, as an aide. She removed herself from the role of buck-stopper, and placed herself in situations that involved working only with children.

    This woman made some drastic life changes so she could remain in the child care field while paying attention to her own needs.

    Pay attention to stress as soon as possible. You may be your own lifesaver.

Sue's Solutions

What Really Works

When I was at the final breaking point, I knew that I had to make some changes in my life or commit myself to a psychiatric ward, so I made these changes:

6   I did what my father told me never to do—I quit my job without having another one.

6   I made a decision to never again wear high heels that could damage my body and cause pain.

6   I found lipstick that would stay on for five hours.

6   I decided that I could shortcut my Clinique three-step facial wash on days when I had to be out of my house before 7 a.m.

6   I began making a winter vacation a priority in my life.

6   I started accumulating toys that offered relief for my stress: slinkies, koosh balls, bubbles, kaleidoscopes, and wands with sparkles in them (Make sure they don't have either Waldo or Elvis hiding in them. They're too stressful to find.).

6   I began collecting humorous cartoons and sayings related to stress. One of my favorites, which I had embossed on a mug, is: "I was put on this earth to accomplish a certain number of things. Right now I'm so far behind, I will never die."

6   I started hanging out with people who appreciated my sense of humor and those who were able to laugh at themselves and others.

Ask Yourself These Questions

No doubt you have found some stress in your life, now let's figure out what to do about it. Ask yourself:

Is the stress I'm experiencing time-limited?
In examining why you are feeling stressed, ask yourself if an end is in sight. For example, if you are working in a supervisory position full-time, have young children at home, and are in school part-time, some of your stress will lessen when your school term is over. Remember that the events in our lives don't cause us stress. The way we react to them does, and how we react to them is under our control.

What kind of stress relievers work for me?
Build in ways to relieve stress during your day. Some of the highly recommended suggestions are: go outside and take a walk around the block; play with a group of babies or toddlers; pretend you are a grandparent; set up a telephone buddy system for problem solving; stash favorite nutritious snacks (or even a limited amount of choco-late) in your desk drawer; turn on a tape or radio station that plays relaxing music; go have lunch with a supportive friend who under-stands you and your job.

Can I recognize my physical and emotional signs of stress?
Stress is different for everyone. I get stressed out when I have to apply makeup for speaking engagements, but I'm not nervous when I face audiences of up to a thousand people. It's vital that you learn to recognize your personal signs of overload and stress: sleep problems, headaches, depression, ulcers, confusion, feeling over-whelmed, and many others which may apply to you.

We often think of stress as something that is happening to us: the roads are icy; dogs are barking when we're trying to deal with an important phone call; or the baby is throwing up on our work clothes just as we're ready to leave the house. All of these situations sound stressful, but in reality it is our reaction to the situation that we need to address.

Some people take situations that seem stressful in stride. When our family flies somewhere, I like to leave early for the airport, allowing time for traffic jams and unforeseen events. My younger daughter likes to arrive at the airport so she has just enough time to run to the gate, hoping that her reserved seat hasn't gone to someone else. She sets herself up for feeling stressed out by allowing no time for mishaps.

To find out how prone you are to feeling stressed, simply answer each of the following questions with either yes or no:

Am I Prone to Stress?

	YES	NO
1. Do I hate to wait?	——	——
2. Do I have a hard time waiting for people to catch up with me, or in lines at the store, or in traffic?	——	——
3. Am I a constant worrier?	——	——
4. Am I overscheduled?	——	——
5. Do I take on more than I can do?	——	——
6. Do I have no time for myself, because I can't say no to others?	——	——
7. Do I over-commit?	——	——
8. Am I unable to take time for myself?	——	——
9. Do I need constant stimulation?	——	——
10. Does silence make me anxious?	——	——
11. Do I consider myself a perfectionist?	——	——
12. Do I strive to be the perfect supervisor, wife, parent, friend, or partner?	——	——
13. Am I harder on myself than others?	——	——
14. Do I rerun conversations in my head?	——	——
15. Do I worry about what people think?	——	——
16. Do I go over how I looked, sounded, or acted?	——	——
Total	——	——

So, how did you do? If you answered yes to six or more questions, then you are susceptible to damaging stress levels. Before you curl up on the couch with a box of chocolates and decide that you are hopeless, and there is no chance for change, please hear this: "There's hope! Yeah!"

You can choose to change your answers to any of the sixteen questions. You can become less prone to feeling stressed out.

Are you still there? Do you believe what I'm saying? We can laugh about uncontrolled stress and deny it, or we can look at the severity of this life-threatening illness and treat it. It's never too late to make positive lifestyle changes in your personal and professional lives.

Summary

We have to assess different situations and determine if what we're dealing with is simply a reaction to a crisis, or a lifestyle pattern. If you are experiencing high levels of stress on a daily basis, stop and ask yourself how long you are going to continue to live your life this way. As the saying goes, "Life is not a dress rehearsal."

I really believe we have the power to control the stress in our lives. It may take something drastic, like quitting a job, or leaving a relationship; but if you believe your life is becoming unmanageable and that you're experiencing more stress than joy, decide to make some changes. Now! Not tomorrow or next week, because if the physical and emotional effects are severe, you may be running out of time.

Don't become passive and helpless. Complete the following Contract For Change, and if necessary, seek professional help.

Personal Contract For Change

After reading the preceding chapter on stress, I am going to make the following changes in my personal and professional lives:

These areas are stressful in my personal life:

    A.

    B.

    C.

To lessen the stress in my personal life I will:

    A.

    B.

    C.

The following areas are stressful in my professional life:

    A.

    B.

    C.

To lessen the stress in my professional life I will·

    A.

    B.

    C.

_____   _____
        signed   date

Lighten Up
And Live Longer

LAUGHTER IS A FORM OF INTERNAL JOGGING.

Self Quiz

As child care professionals we deal with very serious issues daily, and sometimes the intensity can chip away at one's sense of humor. Take a few minutes to check yes or no on the following statements:

	YES	NO
1. People have told me that I seem more serious lately.	——	——
2. I used to laugh more than I do now.	——	——
3. I feel less tolerant of parents and other staff with whom I work.	——	——
4. I don't go out of my way to remember funny stories that I hear from the children.	——	——
5. I have difficulty finding humor in serious things.	——	——
6. I don't think humor and laughter help anything.	——	——
7. I grew up in a very serious environment where humor was not part of daily life.	——	——
8. I would say that I have very high personal standards, and it's difficult for me to laugh at my own mistakes.	——	——
9. I believe that we can't control our emotions. They just happen.	——	——
10. My job is very demanding with not much room for laughter.	——	——
Total	——	——

If you checked yes on four or more of the above statements, you are definitely in need of a laughter break. By reading the rest of this chapter, you will gather more information about the positive side of developing a sense of humor. Keep reading. My hope is that you'll soon be able to smile more and live longer.

Survival Tips

1. Develop and maintain personal relationships with people who know how to have fun.

2. Take time away from your office to spend with the children in your program.

3. Call someone on the phone, and tell them you need to hear something humorous.

4. Rent or go see a funny movie.

5. Read the comic section of the newspaper.

6. Play with a puppy or a kitten.

7. Shift gears. Take the focus away from what is causing you to feel uptight or stressed.

8. Rock a toddler or a baby.

9. Leave your environment and go for a walk with a friend.

10. Take a vacation.

11. Listen to the child inside you who needs to laugh and play.

12. Go buy a bottle of bubbles (or make your own) and keep them in your car to use during traffic jams.

13. Share a funny story about the children from your program.

14. Ask the children in your program to bring in something to share that makes them laugh.

15. Allow yourself to be silly.

16. Laugh with, instead of at, others ("That reminds me of the time I....").

Sue's Solutions

What Really Works

⑥ Laughter is nonfattening, contagious, and a tranquilizer without the side affects. We can't even use the excuse "I can't afford it," because a sense of humor is free and accessible most hours of the day or night.

⑥ Laughter does the body good. When we laugh we are releasing endorphins, which are feel-good chemicals. We are also suppressing the output of adrenaline, which is a stress inducing hormone.

⑥ Laughter gives us a different perspective on life. When we are in serious climates and relationships, we tend to walk around wearing a doom and gloom face. Remember, one of the intangible benefits of working in a child care program is, if we take the time, we'll notice that the children are laughing and having fun all day. Fun can become contagious, if we choose to let it.

⑥ Developing and maintaining a sense of humor has many benefits including:

- breaking tension;
- providing a useful release tool when things are getting intense;
- functioning as a helpful strategy against defensive people;
- reducing embarrassment;
- keeping us balanced;
- working as a coping mechanism.

⑥ Comedy is simply a funny way of being serious. Have you ever listened to people who are adept at taking a serious incident and turning it into something humorous? It's best to do this when we are talking about ourselves.

When I tell friends some of the humorous experiences I've had because of my poor cooking talents, they laugh at the stories. Their amazement when I show up with good, edible food for a potluck adds to the fun.

6 As child care professionals, we are very good at encouraging the children we are with on a daily basis to laugh and have fun. What about the child within each of us? We need to remember the childlike characteristics we had as a child, and maintain these as adults, no matter what our age.

6 Well-placed humor can create a different, and less stressful perception of a problem. Again, we have to be careful not to resort to humor in situations that need to remain serious. But humor has a time and a place, and it can often help lighten up a situation.

6 Sharing ourselves reveals our character. Don't be afraid to tell stories about yourself. It's usually easier to find something humorous in a serious situation after the fact, and it's okay to laugh at ourselves.

6 When someone takes a risk by sharing humor, that person's giving you a gift. Not everyone is good at telling jokes or making people laugh. So when they try, offer them encouragement.

6 Learn, and then, teach others the difference between good and toxic humor. Not all humor works. Sarcastic humor, racist or sexist jokes, or laughter at another's expense, are not acceptable. When we hear others taking part in hurtful humor, we need to be assertive and say something. "I don't think what you said is funny or appropriate" is simple and straightforward.

6 We don't have to be prisoners of our feelings. We can learn to recognize our feelings once we are in touch with them. We can, to some extent, control them. Research tells us when we're happy, we smile. We don't smile first. Sometimes, we have to purposely laugh or smile, and when we act first, sometimes the feelings follow.

6 The ability to laugh at ourselves is the bridge between an unhealthy need to be perfect and positive mental health. Perfectionists find it difficult to be gentle with themselves and to learn from their mistakes.

As much as some people don't want to either hear the statement, or admit that it's true, the fact is: no person is perfect. We are human, and we need to learn to lighten up.

6 Humans are the only life form that laughs. Laughing is a coping mechanism that can help us tolerate pain. Laughter is sometimes appropriate when we feel that we need to get over self-imposed sadness. At other times, we need to deal with the pain that we may try to disguise with humor.

6 "When laughter goes–there goes civilization," said Erma Bombeck, a great comic writer, who died the day I was writing this chapter. How ironic that I would be writing a chapter about humor on the day when someone I deeply admire, and whose humorous writing added so much to our civilization, died.

We should remember her words and quote them to other people we think should be less serious and intense.

6 I make a point of reading the cartoons daily to find material that might help me and others laugh. As I said previously, research tells us that three to five minutes of laughter, or a hundred belly laughs, can double our heart rate–the aerobic affect equivalent to ten strenuous minutes on a rowing machine.

6 Think about this quote from John F. Kennedy: "There are three things that are real–God, human folly, and laughter. The first two are beyond comprehension. So, we must do what we can with the third."

Ask Yourself These Questions

What do I have to gain by laughing at myself?

When we are able to laugh at ourselves, we give others permission to also laugh, and we share a little of ourselves. Laughing at oneself is a great technique to use with children, because it helps teach them how to develop a sense of humor.

Why is it easier for me to get caught up in the intensity of this career?

As child care professionals our work influences children's lives and their future. It's difficult to find or use humor in situations where we are dealing with dysfunctional families, apathetic parents, or staff who don't share our concern for professionalism. I'm not suggesting that we walk around laughing all day, but I do recommend the positive aspects of humor previously listed in this chapter.

How can I use the material in this chapter with the children?

Children learn best by seeing and doing. Here are some ways of incorporating humor into your child care program:

- Read funny stories to the children.

- Have a "Smile" day and ask children to bring something from home that is funny.

- Show videos of some of our great comedians.

- Teach children the difference between toxic and good humor.

- Let the children see you smile and laugh.

- Have a column in your newsletter called "Kids Say the Funniest Things."

Summary

The topics of humor and laughter aren't usually discussed in articles or in books on child development. I hope you can now see the necessity of addressing humor to create balance with the intensity of our jobs.

Here are some quotes from men and women about humor and laughter. I hope they bring a smile to your face. If you enjoy them, pass them on to others. We can all use more humor in our lives.

Something To Think About

"She who laughs, lasts!"
– Mary Pettibone Poole

6

"Comedy is simply a funny way of being serious."
– unknown

6

"The sense of humor has other things to do
than make itself conspicuous in the act of laughter."
– Alice Meynell

6

"Laughter is the shortest distance between two people."
– Victor Borge

6

"You don't have to teach people to be funny.
You only have to give them permission."
Dr. Harvey Mindess

6

"Humor brings insight and tolerance."
– Agnes Repplier

6

"The art of medicine consists of amusing the patient
while nature cures the disease."
– Voltaire

6

"Live to love" was my father's motto:
"Live to laugh," is mine.
— *Hannah Cowley*

❻

"Death is nature's way of telling us to slow down."
— *unknown*

❻

"To get them listening . . . get them laughing."
— *Allen Klein*

❻

"Laugh and the world laughs with you;
Weep, and you weep alone."
— *Ella Wheeler Wilcox*

❻

"You don't stop laughing because you grow old,
you grow old because you stop laughing."
— *Michael Pritchard*

❻

"Those who do not know how to weep with their
whole heart don't know how to laugh either."
— *Golda Meir*

❻

"People will pay more to be entertained
than to be educated."
— *Johnny Carson*

❻

"You grow up the day you have
your first real laugh at yourself."
– *Ethel Barrymore*

6

"Laughter interrupts the panic cycle of an illness."
– *Norman Cousins*

6

"Exaggeration is the cheapest form of humor."
– *Elizabeth Peters*

6

"Have Fun–Misery is Optional"
– *Bumper Sticker*

Personal Contract For Change

After reading the preceding chapter on the importance of developing and maintaining a sense of humor, I'm willing to make the following changes:

I will develop and use these positive affirmations related to the positive effects of humor:

A.

B.

C.

I will incorporate these survival tips into my routine at work and at home:

A.

B.

C.

I will encourage the staff and parents to develop and use a sense of humor by:

A.

B.

C.

I will teach the children about humor by doing the following:

A.

B.

C.

_____   _____

          signed   date

Communicating Is More Than Just Talking

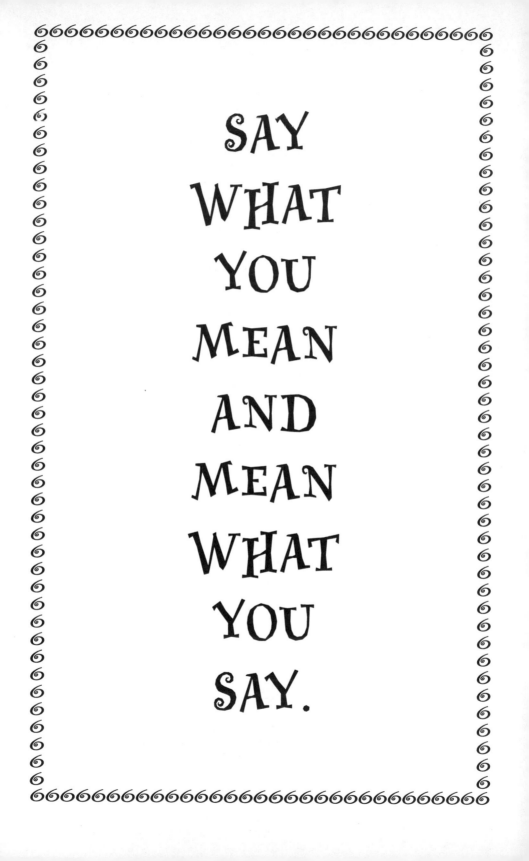

SAY
WHAT
YOU
MEAN
AND
MEAN
WHAT
YOU
SAY.

Self Quiz

Communicating effectively with others is an essential skill for all child care managers and their staff. This self quiz will help you assess your various styles of communicating. Check yes or no after each statement.

	YES	NO
1. Sometimes it seems as though no matter how much I talk, others are not listening to me.	___	___
2. When I'm nervous, I speak more quickly.	___	___
3. I have difficulty finding time for uninterrupted conversations.	___	___
4. Sometimes I forget to pay attention to non-verbal cues.	___	___
5. Frequent distractions make it difficult for me to give my undivided attention to listening.	___	___
6. When some people are speaking to me, I become impatient and find myself finishing their sentences.	___	___
7. I become very frustrated with parents when they don't read the information we send home with them.	___	___
8. I sometimes become defensive when someone is saying something I don't want to hear.	___	___
9. I used to think that I knew how to communicate, but now I'm having doubts.	___	___
10. I have a difficult time communicating with others when I'm angry or upset.	___	___
Total	___	___

If you checked yes after three or more of the above statements, read on. This chapter will help you sharpen your communication skills, which include listening and paying attention to other people. Even if you didn't have three yes answers, the chapter will help you say what you mean and get your message heard.

Survival Tips

1. For important communication, set aside special time.

2. Don't assume that others understand what you are saying. Ask questions that will tell you if clarification is needed.

3. Use "I" messages to help lower the other person's defensiveness.

4. Do not lecture, preach or "should" at another person.

5. Practice your own listening skills.

6. With persistent people, use the broken-record technique. Repeat and repeat.

7. Use active listening skills and train staff to do the same.

8. Use and maintain eye contact throughout a conversation.

9. Don't be afraid of silence. Don't fill the air with idle chatter.

10. Let other people know how you value them.

11. When appropriate, set up another time to readdress the issue that's under discussion.

12. Try varying forms of communication: notes, telephone calls, newsletters, and bulletin boards; and become creative with your variations.

13. Don't fake listening. If you are distracted and cannot give the other person your full attention, schedule a time to talk. Otherwise you might say something you didn't intend to say, because you weren't able to fully listen.

14. Be aware of non-verbal cues from other people–if they fold their arms, glare at you, avoid eye contact, or clench their fists and/or jaws–change your technique.

15. Practice and use two-way communication. Lecturing, ordering, and demanding are not effective forms of communication.

Sue's Solutions

What Really Works

∽ We have two ears, but only one mouth, for a reason. We can learn more from listening than continuous talking. When we speak we are usually saying things we already know, but when we listen we might learn something new. What someone says to us is just as important as what we have to say to them.

∽ Listening saves time. When we actively listen we make fewer mistakes, fewer interpersonal misunderstandings occur, and we can develop better long-term relationships. Poor listening is a habit we can change.

∽ *Active listening* is a technique that acknowledges to other people that you're hearing what they have to say. Use this skill when you want to build a relationship, not when you are having a brief encounter. Active listening is useful when listening to a child, parent, or other staff member. However, it isn't necessary when you're ordering a meal at a restaurant. Keep the following tips in mind, when you are actively listening:

- Maintain eye contact.
- Use verbal responses such as "really," "uh-huh," or "go on."
- Use non-verbal messages: smile, nod your head, or lean forward with interest.
- Ask questions or restate the statement to clarify points in the conversation.

∽ When child care staff and providers become frustrated talking with parents, the reason is usually a communication gap. For example, sometimes we say or request something and get no response. Here are some helpful, creative ways to bridge that gap and communicate with parents:

- *Newsletters:* Consistently include input from staff, parents, and other community agencies to make the task less time consuming. The results will be more interesting, too.

- *Log Book:* A simple spiral notebook in each classroom will let parents communicate about their children so that staff, who work different shifts, will be able to read comments such as: "Our family dog, Bouser, died last night and Olivia is having a hard time."

  Another log book can be in the office for notes to staff from other classrooms such as: "Pat Rodriquez will pick up Paul at 10:00 this morning for a dentist appointment."

- *Bulletin Boards:* In each of the classrooms and hallways bulletin boards can provide a place for children's decorations, their art work, and flyers about different community, school, and program events.

- *White Boards:* Available in various sizes, white boards are easily erased and are excellent for writing notes to parents and receiving notes from them: "Reminder: Field trip to the zoo tomorrow. Bring a bag lunch." You can also promote positive events such as birthdays, and send thank you notes between staff and parents.

- *Diapers:* No, this is not a error or misspelling. A creative way to get a message home to parents of children in diapers is to write a note on the diaper with a magic marker (before you diaper the child) to let the parent know their supply needs replenishing. "I need more diapers" should help get the message home. Supplement this communication with a written note and a verbal reminder.

- *Daily Notes:* Notes are particularly useful for parents with children who are non-verbal. Keeping these notes simple and focused more on positive events than negative behavior is important. Parents with infants and toddlers may want to know about their daily eating and bathroom routines.

- *Telephone Calls:* New parents in your program may want to call and check to see how their children did with the morning transition; a brief telephone call may give them needed assurance.

- *Pagers:* For parents who use them at work, pagers provide immediate contact if their child is sick or injured.

☺ Log books and white boards are also effective ways of communicating among staff. The material recorded in the log book can serve as a form of documentation and contains information that all staff needs to know. "The staff meeting agenda is posted in the staff lounge. Please add your agenda topics to the list."

Requesting that staff initial the items they have read, assures that they've seen your message. Information on white boards can be temporary and erased when no longer needed. For example, "Pay checks will be ready at 10 a.m. on Friday."

☺ Important communications need undivided attention and shouldn't take place outside on the playground or by the cubbies. Find a space away from general activities, and set aside a time that allows for uninterrupted communication.

☺ Be aware of feeling defensive. When people say things to us that are painful to hear, such as criticism, it's not unusual to feel the need to protect ourselves. Try to stay open to hearing the comments. If this isn't possible, the problem may lie in how the other person is delivering the message.

It's okay to say, "I'm feeling defensive right now as you're speaking." That may stop the way the conversation is progressing, and allow for focusing on how the message is being sent and received.

☺ Use "I" messages. When I first heard about this technique many years ago, I thought the reference was to "eye" messages, and that I was supposed to change the way I was looking at the other person—a good example of miscommunication. Use the "I" formula when delivering a message to others:

- I feel _____
- When you _____
- Because _____

"I feel angry *when you* are late for work *because* that puts more pressure on me to go into the classroom and takes me away from doing my job in the office."

At first you might feel awkward using this technique, but I assure you that it does work and does help lessen the need to feel defensive.

6 Keep focused on the positive, and encourage others to do the same. Send short notes of appreciation to staff or parents. "Thanks so much for coming on the field trip with us to the zoo. We appreciate you taking the time and Ronda seemed to enjoy having her father with her for the morning."

6 Constructive criticism and feedback should benefit the receiver. This isn't the time to say something that will hurt or offend the other person. "I thought the children seemed restless during group time. You might want to consider reading a shorter story tomorrow."

6 Avoid using words that have fuzzy or unclear meanings. Words like "always," "never," "often," and "a lot" are just a few that don't offer a true description of what you're trying to say. Be brief, but very specific, so you get your point across. Which sentence is clearer to understand? "We never have fire drills anymore." Or "We have missed the last four fire drills."

6 Use assertive communication skills to make your point:

- Be clear, brief, and specific.

- Use and maintain eye contact.

- Ask for what you want or need.

- Don't try to manipulate the other person by using questions rather than statements.

- Use appropriate, but not forceful, non-verbal messages.

- Use a firm, but not angry, voice.

- Don't blame, condone, or lecture the other person.

6 A director who attended one of my training sessions mailed me the following saying:

"People don't get along because they fear each other. People fear each other because they don't know each other. They don't know each other because they have not properly communicated with each other." – Martin Luther King, Jr.

Ask Yourself These Questions

How can I handle persistent people who do not seem to be listening to me?

The broken-record technique, which I referred to earlier, works with persistent people. For example, it would have been very effective when I was trying to communicate with my daughter, Carrie, when she was a teenager.

Carrie was not receptive to hearing me when I turned down a request. She would ask. I would refuse. She would continue to ask, demand, question, and badger until I gave in and said what she wanted to hear.

The broken-record technique consists of stating repeatedly what you want in a calm, direct manner with the persistence of a broken record. When you use this technique, you stay focused on what you want and don't give in to the other person's will. You simply state what you want as many times as you need to, without changing your mind.

This technique is not designed to foster a relationship, but rather to get what you want with a minimum of communication. Here is an example of using it with a staff person who is being persistent:

Staff: Can I come in late for work tomorrow?

Manager: No. We are already short staffed and I need you here at 8:00 in the morning.

Staff: What if I get someone to cover my shift?

Manager: No. I need you here tomorrow.

Staff: Can I come in late if I promise to work late in the afternoon?

Manager: No. You need to be here at 8:00 tomorrow.

I try to be assertive in my communication, but I have difficulty getting my point across. Is there something else I need to consider?

If you find people are responding to your assertive request with any of the following:

- changing the subject;

- responding with a strong display of emotion (including anger);
- making fun of your request;
- trying to make you feel guilty about your request;
- criticizing or questioning the legitimacy of your request;
- asking you why you want what you asked for;

they are, in all probability, trying to manipulate you. Be persistent and use techniques such as the broken record to overcome their attempts to avoid or discount what you're saying.

Am I *really* able to concentrate on what the other person is saying to me?
Your job is not always conducive to uninterrupted conversations, so it's important to be honest with other people if you aren't able to focus 100% on what they're saying. An appropriate response might be, "I'm distracted by several things that need my attention right now. I'd like to set up a time to talk when we can do so without interruptions."

Summary

The topic of communication is very important and complex. Communication is an integral part of every chapter of this book and weaves throughout all of our interpersonal relationships. Hundreds of publications delve into this topic in more detail, and I would recommend that you go to the library, or to a bookstore, for more information.

As child care managers, we are role models for the children and adults with whom we have contact. We must be able to communicate, to listen, and to teach others to acquire similar skills. Spend time working on this topic, and understand that it's a daily, ongoing process.

Personal Contract For Change

After reading the chapter on communication, I'm going to make the following changes:

I will begin overcoming these roadblocks to effective communication:

     A.

     B.

     C.

I will begin using *active listening* skills with the following people at the following times:

Person	When
A.	A.
B.	B.
C.	C.

If I think I'm being manipulated, I will check for the following signs:

     A.

     B.

     C.

     D.

I will start or continue communicating with staff/parents by using log books, and the other tools listed below:

     A.

     B.

     C.

_____   _____

          signed   date

Building A
Better Team

FEW BURDENS ARE HEAVY WHEN EVERYONE LIFTS.

Self Quiz

One of the main roles of a child care manager or supervisor is that of coach to the teaching staff. Think of your current attitude, and your role as supervisor, as you take this self quiz on team building. Check yes or no after each statement.

	YES	NO
1. I currently have some concerns about how staff is operating as a team.	___	___
2. People are not communicating well or listening to each other.	___	___
3. Conflict is not being effectively resolved among staff.	___	___
4. Currently there is (or has been lately) a problem with staff morale.	___	___
5. Some staff don't feel that they are being treated fairly.	___	___
6. Constructive feedback among staff is lacking at this time.	___	___
7. Our staff meetings seem to be less effective than I would like them to be.	___	___
8. We are currently experiencing a lot of staff turnover.	___	___
9. There seems to be more competition than collaboration between individuals and classroom staffs.	___	___
10. Our staff members used to work together as a team better than they do now.	___	___
Total	___	___

Building and maintaining an effective team is a priority, so this chapter is a must-read for any child care manager. If you checked yes to three or fewer statements, you are doing well as a team builder, but read the chapter for a review.

Survival Tips

1. Each time you have a turnover of staff, keep the team concept in mind when you are filling the vacancy.

2. A staff vacancy may be the time to shift various team members to create a more balanced group of professionals.

3. When doing an orientation session with the staff, make sure they understand the goals and philosophy of the program.

4. Pay attention to staff morale, which is the same as keeping your finger on the pulse of your staff.

5. Encourage healthy conflict (see Chapter 9 on Little Spats and Huge Disputes) among staff members.

6. Bring a consultant into your program to teach all staff effective communication skills. The goal you are working toward is openness and honesty among staff. This is an on-going process you will need to address frequently at regular staff meetings and in-service training sessions.

7. Be aware of all the different teams within your one program (rooms, positions, different shifts, management, and other groupings). Draw diagrams of all the teams and display them, maybe with cute sayings attached to the diagrams.

8. Consult with the staff on important decisions such as making changes to the building or restructuring the benefit package. This involvement can help promote ownership of the program.

9. Use regularly scheduled staff meetings as a time to build a better team. Plan events which promote collaboration among staff from different classrooms.

10. When problems arise in the program, move quickly to address and resolve them.

11. Treat each team member as an individual, focusing on each person's strengths and minimizing each person's weaknesses.

12. Balance work and social activities for staff so they can get to know their other team members as individuals.

13. Train staff how to give each other effective feedback and constructive criticism by role modeling with them on a daily basis. Also work on these skills in staff meetings.

14. Encourage individual members of a team to take initiative and become leaders for those who need to follow. Experienced staff could be mentors for new team members.

15. If you are working with a board of directors, spend some training time with the board and staff, working together on team-building skills. These sessions will enable each group to learn more about the other.

16. Semi-annually, have the teams do a self-assessment.

17. Encourage, through your own example, acceptance of others' accomplishments and mistakes.

18. Support collaboration rather than competition among various teams within your program by having people from different classrooms form new teams for special projects. For example, select one member from each classroom team to form the plan ning committee when a special event is on the program's agenda.

Sue's Solutions

What Really Works

6 Respecting each other's strengths and weaknesses is a key
   ingredient for a successful team. Some people are leaders, some
   followers. Some people are flexible, some are more structured
   in their approach to their work. Some love working with babies,
   while others are better at dealing with parents. Many kinds of
   people are needed as team players in a child care program.
   Diversity is really the name of the game. Your role as program
   manager is to get, and keep, these people working together as a
   team.

6 Just like a coach on a professional sports team, you want to
   assemble the best players. You want to work with them so they
   know how to blend and collaborate, rather than compete with
   each other. When an opening takes place on your staff, reassess
   your various teams. See if some internal shifting of existing staff
   would enhance your program before you start the hiring process
   for a new person.

6 When I asked a group of child care professionals to describe the
   necessary qualities of team members within their programs,
   they came up with the following words and/or phrases:

sensitivity	non-judgmental	consistent
non-competitive	high commitment	pride in work
positive strokes	positive attitude	trust
patience with others	sense of humor	honesty
understanding of differences		openness

   Try this exercise with your staff. See if you can come up with
   other descriptive words.

6 If problems exist within a certain team, you can check to see if
   they are clear about what each of their roles is. All staff needs to
   know what is expected of them as team players. A continuous

assessment process needs to be in place. When a shift in players (staff members) happens, check to see if a shift in roles is needed.

6 Here is a quick self-assessment that each staff member can answer. Check yes or no after the following statements:

	YES	NO
1. I know our team goals.	___	___
2. Our team enjoys working together.	___	___
3. Every member plays a role on our team.	___	___
4. Our team members listen to each other without judgment.	___	___
5. We use problem-solving skills to resolve conflict.	___	___
6. Everyone supports the outcome of a decision.	___	___
7. Team members are dependable, cooperative, and candid.	___	___
8. All team members fulfill their share of responsibilities.	___	___
9. We all share in the leadership of the team.	___	___
10. We appreciate each other's diverse style.	___	___
Total	___	___

Good teams assess their effectiveness every so often to see where they were, where they are, and where they're going.

6 Read the saying on the following page. It sums up what working as a team is all about. You can copy and display the saying in a staff lounge or in another area where everyone can read and comment on what it says:

> Coming together
> is a beginning.
>
> Keeping together
> is progress.
>
> Working together
> is success.

Ask Yourself These Questions

How can I tell if I need an outside consultant to help me with team building?

Although building and maintaining a team is an ongoing job, you might want to consider having a consultant if you seem stuck with a particular problem. Think of programs as a family, with the manager or director as the parent. When families get stuck, they often seek advice, support, or help from outside sources.

How am I encouraging teams to act interdependently of each other?

Draw a picture of the entire program and of the various teams. Let personnel see how the teams look on paper. Talk about how they are all separate, but working toward one common goal–the well-being of the total program.

Teams act independently from each other on some projects, but they also work together on activities such as fundraisers, special holiday events, and program open houses.

How can I encourage sensitivity towards new staff members on the team?

Before the new staff person begins, openly discuss the benefits of this person's capabilities and skills. Encourage discussion about any resistance to changing the team that people might have. Then, listen.

People need to be able to speak their fears, and know that they are heard. When new staff members arrive, take time to bring them into the group. Also, provide the new person with a mentor who has been working in the program for some time.

When a staff vacancy occurs, I feel this sense of urgency to fill the position. How can I slow down and wait to assess the current team?

For a temporary solution, to give yourself some time, you might consider doing one of the following: 1) Fill in for a while to assess the current team and see first-hand what shifting needs to take place. 2) Hire a substitute to work in the room until you make a decision. 3) Have a meeting with the lead teachers for each room and ask for their suggestions.

We tend to panic when a vacancy arises, and we jump in to fix the problem rather than evaluate what the best solution will be for all concerned.

How can I make the most of the limited time we have for staff meetings?

Here are some tips for successful meetings which will also help strengthen the various teams within your program:

- Post the agenda two weeks before the meeting.

- Encourage staff to add their items of concern to the agenda.

- Encourage or mandate that everyone on staff attend meetings. Pay your staff to be there, and offer food.

- Let various staff members lead the meeting.

- Add in-service training after the business meeting.

- Encourage various staff members to do some of the training. For example, members could share what they learned at a conference they recently attended.

- Use a timed agenda with a pre-posted starting and ending time.

- Add sucessful tips to this list that have worked for your program.

Summary

Team building is a craft that begins on the first day the program is open and is essential every day. It affects each person who works in the program; and parents, children, and the community will benefit from the important work of an effective team.

When I do team-building training for programs, we end the session with an exercise called "The Ball of Yarn." Staff members form a circle. Each person takes a turn holding onto a piece of the yarn, then throws the ball to another staff member. The person who throws the yarn tells the member who catches it of a quality he or she appreciates about that person. For example, "I appreciate your sense of humor during times of crises." At the conclusion of this exercise, all staff members are holding onto the yarn, creating a web, which links them together as a total team.

An effective team is like this web of yarn—each person needed and appreciated by other staff members. When people are not there to hold up their part of the web, their absence is noticed, and they are missed.

The goal of continuous team building is to create a strong and effective staff who can hold together through good and bad times. Individual members of the team may change, but the team remains whole and supportive; and members trust each other.

Personal Contract For Change

After reading the chapter on building a better team, I'm going to make the following changes:

I will focus on the diverse styles in each of our teams looking for the following qualities:

A.	D.
B.	E.
C.	F.

I will assume the responsibility for developing and maintaining effective teams, and I will call in a consultant when the following problems are occurring:

A.

B.

C.

When a staff vacancy occurs, I will take the following steps before immediately hiring someone new:

A.

B.

C.

I'm going to work on training the staff to use the following skills related to being an effective team player:

A.

B.

C.

D.

_____   _____
            signed   date

Teaming with Parents

KIDS
DON'T
COME
WITH A
SET OF
INSTRUCTIONS.

Self Quiz

Parents are an integral part of the child care program team. Take this brief quiz to see how well you and your staff are doing with developing good parent relations. Mark yes or no after each statement:

	YES	NO
1. I have doubts about the parenting skills of many of the parents.	___	___
2. Some of the parents place unachievable demands on the staff.	___	___
3. Many of the parents refuse to show appreciation to their children's teachers.	___	___
4. I question if there is a match between my program goals and several of the parents' expectations.	___	___
5. The parents I work with seem overextended and stressed out.	___	___
6. The teachers complain that parents are not reading notes.	___	___
7. I am experiencing problems with overbearing parents.	___	___
8. Some of the parents are confused about appropriate developmental stages for their children.	___	___
9. Parents are questioning their children's teachers' capabilities.	___	___
10. I am dealing with parents who aren't abiding by the program policies.	___	___
Total	___	___

If you marked yes after one or more of the above statements, I advise you to read more about how you can build positive relationships with parents. The value of positive parent relationships can't be ignored. Happy reading.

Survival Tips

1. Introduce the parents to their child's prospective teaching staff before the child starts the program.

2. Ask parents if they have any specific questions about the information in the handbooks.

3. Ask parents to initial a sign-off document stating that they read *and* understood the items in the parent handbook.

4. Spend time training staff on issues of working with parents. These issues should be high on your priority list of training musts.

5. Remind staff that, although they may spend more time with some children than the parents do, they must respect the parents' rights and concerns.

6. Decide who is the most appropriate person to speak with parents about their child's reoccurring problems. Choices could include the teacher, director, or a specialist.

7. Respect parents' diversity.

8. Put limits and boundaries in writing so that parents know what can and cannot be discussed about other children or about confidential issues.

9. Encourage parents to show their appreciation to the program staff by writing notes to the staff or relaying positive comments in the parents' log book. A suggestion might be: "Thanks for planning the great field trip. Josh loved playing with the animals."

10. Seek out parents who appear to be advocates of the program to serve on either the Board of Directors or the Parent Advisory Committee.

11. Solicit parents to donate their time and talents to help in your program in areas such as typing the newsletter, going on field trips, and bringing birthday treats.

12. Inform parents, during orientation, that children will learn some things (such as swear words) and do some things (maybe get dirty or get hurt) that they won't approve of. Tell them their children will also learn positive things such as how to relate to other adults and children, how to speak their feelings rather than act them out, and how to share with others.

13. Encourage parents to check out stories their children bring home from your program. Tell them that you will also let them know about any issues of concern the children might be reporting from home.

14. Remember that, almost without exception, parents love their children and want what's best for them.

15. Children feel insecure if they think their parents and caregivers don't like each other. Caution staff to *never* talk negatively about parents in front of the children.

Sue's Solutions

What Really Works

Whenever I talk with directors and managers about their programs, the topic of parents comes into the discussion. "I have a great group of parents this year," might be one of the comments a teacher will make, or another might say, "I love working with the children, but the parents are driving me crazy." Here are some tips that child care managers have used that actually work:

6 A good match between the parents and the program is essential. I encourage parents to spend a great amount of time choosing the child care program that will meet their needs. This is when I wish price fixing was legal and parents would make their choice of a child care program based on quality rather than cost. Parents should make an appointment to meet with the director to learn about the philosophy of the program and to see the physical environment.

6 Introduce the parents to their child's prospective teaching staff. All parents (and their children) should have an opportunity to meet the team of staff members who will be working in the classroom. Due to varying schedules, they may not be able to meet all of the team, but introductions to the primary staff are a must.

6 One of the most difficult skills that child care professionals need to learn is respecting parents. Sometimes providers think (and occasionally their thoughts are justified) that they are spending more time with the children than the parents spend with them. Regardless of that, the parents have the final word in the upbringing of their children. We are there to support parents, not to take over their role.

6 Some parents are not yet skilled at developmentally appropriate practices (DAP) and need coaching as to when the child will do certain self-help skills. When an excited toddler parent comes in requesting that her fourteen month old start potty training, we

need to support the parent; but, also, we need to inform her, gently and professionally, about when it is appropriate to begin toilet training. Please caution staff to avoid becoming flippant and sarcastic when parents make what seem to be unreasonable requests.

⑥ Parents who want to begin new developmental skills such as potty training should be encouraged to start the new endeavor on a weekend. The teacher can continue working with the child throughout the week.

This schedule is more likely to assure continuity, because the parents are ready to begin the process; and they'll be more apt to follow through the next weekend.

⑥ Praise and encouragement are necessary for parents as well as children. When parents, who normally rush as they drop off their child in the morning, take extra time one morning to deal with a child's clinging, say something positive to them as they leave or when they return that evening. "Thanks for your patience this morning with Paul. He calmed down almost immediately after you left. The time you spent seemed to make a difference with him."

⑥ When parents are coming to your program after a long day at work, the last thing they want to hear from you or other staff is what a rotten day their child had. Encourage your staff to put themselves in the parents' shoes. As parents how would they like to be bombarded with bad news?

Some programs use written daily reports, particularly for infants and toddlers, and focus on the positives as well as mentioning some of the disasters. Weigh your words and decide which issues are really important enough to discuss.

⑥ Telling parents that their child is not fitting in with your program is one of the most trying tasks that you, as a manager, will have to face. Sometimes you may need to refer children to another program, either in another center or a home. This conversation is very difficult to have with parents. I would advise practicing the conversation with another professional before the actual meeting.

The well-being of all the children in the program may be the most important issue, but the one child you must terminate is the focus of the discussion. Go into this meeting prepared with your recommendations for future child care and under what circumstances you would give the child another chance. For example, if the parents agree to begin counseling by a certain date, you could agree to reevaluate in thirty days.

6   One of the key ingredients for building and continuing a positive relationship with parents is effective communication. I've devoted Chapter 6 of this book to communication, and I recommend that you refer to it for tips on enhancing your communication with parents.

6   I have a cartoon that shows a little boy sitting on the ground with his blanket, saying, "Our new child care provider is twenty-two and doesn't have any kids. She wants us to call her 'Auntie April.' I give her two days, maybe three at the max."

    I think the over-zealous teacher, young or old, who wants to be called by a specific title might be offensive to some parents or school age children. You probably have single, twenty-two-year-old people working for you. They need to be respected as professionals and not put down for being who they are. Parents need to be educated about the training that all child care professionals have prior to employment, and that they continue to get on an ongoing basis.

6   I had a personal experience where a teacher who worked for me was very critical of parents, because they forgot important things such as extra clothes, boots in the winter, and swim suits for water play activities.

    Then, she became a parent. She started forgetting important things for her children and became much more tolerant of the parents she worked with. The key factor here is to encourage staff—whether they do or do not have children of their own— and parents to respect each other.

6   Parent education is a necessity. Some states have specialized state departments that deal specifically with parenting issues. If you would like to offer ongoing classes for your parents, you

might incorporate family nights that include pizza or box lunches, free child care, and parenting classes on topics and issues relevant to your program.

I'm sure, for instance, parents of toddlers would be grateful to learn more about biting. Parents of preschoolers could learn more about redirecting negative behavior; and parents of schoolagers would be grateful to learn that spitting, scratching, and swearing are sometimes age-appropriate behavior.

Ask Yourself These Questions

What can I do with parents who are late and not respectful of our closing time?

I am a firm believer in late fees as a consequence for parents who don't pick up their children on time. Many child care professionals are hesitant to charge parents more money.

However, incorporating late fees into your program policies will tell your parents that their tardiness is not acceptable to you. Chronic lateness may be grounds for termination from the program.

Be sure that you have backed up your actions with the written policies the parents have all read and agreed to.

Am I supportive of the parents' values that are different from our program's values?

We need to respect parents' diversity and the style in which they raise their children. We can team with parents when it comes to a particular situation, for example, discipline, by asking them how they handle a given situation at home.

If they admit that they haven't had much success, then we can offer suggestions of methods that work while the child is in our program. Licensed programs must abide by certain values such as not spanking a child or not withholding food from a child. Respecting values can be a delicate issue and often one of compromise.

How do I respond to parents who want us to spank their child?

Check with your state or county regulations, but most child care programs *forbid* the spanking of children. You can offer the parents a bit of education by informing them that research shows that children who are spanked don't learn how to resolve conflicts without using physical violence.

Offer parents alternative suggestions to spanking such as redirecting a child's behavior, or conflict-resolution techniques. Team with parents on the type of discipline that you both can use and evaluate the progress frequently.

Summary

Building and enhancing positive relationships with the parents in your program can be time consuming and sometimes frustrating; however, the rewards can be worth the effort. Relationship building begins the first time parents come into your school, center, or home and continues until their last day with you.

It takes a whole-team approach to build positive relationships and to build a program in which parents and providers work together for what's best for the children.

Personal Contract For Change

After reading the tips offered in this chapter on teaming with parents, I plan to work on the following issues:

I will work on these three survival tips, and create a plan for training other staff:

     A.

     B.

     C.

I will do the following things to build an effective parents/staff team:

     A.

     B.

     C.

I will encourage parents to attend training sessions on the following topics:

     A.

     B.

     C.

I will offer training sessions for my staff on the following topics:

     A.

     B.

     C.

_____   _____

        signed   date

Little Spats
and Huge
Disputes

DISAGREEMENTS DO NOT HAVE TO TURN INTO CONFLICT.

Self Quiz

Conflict among adults who work in or use a child care program is inevitable. How we deal with it is what's important. Please take the following self quiz about conflict and check either the yes or no column for each statement:

	YES	NO
1. It's hard for me to stand up for myself during a confrontation.	___	___
2. I have a hard time expressing my feelings during conflict.	___	___
3. I become intimidated when others express their anger toward me.	___	___
4. I would rather avoid conflict than work it out.	___	___
5. After a confrontation, I need space from the other person for a long time.	___	___
6. Trusting the other person is difficult after a confrontation.	___	___
7. At our program, there seems to be a lot of tension, frustration, and misunderstandings.	___	___
8. I feel defensive when someone comes to me with a conflict.	___	___
9. As a child, I didn't see conflict resolution modeled by adults.	___	___
10. I feel like an easy target with aggressive and manipulative adults.	___	___
Total	___	___

If you checked yes to four on more of the above statements, immediately read this chapter on conflict resolution. The next time you find yourself in a conflict situation, you'll be able keep your cool and stand your ground.

Survival Tips

1. When dealing with adults who are feuding, refer to techniques used with children such as encouraging those involved to handle it themselves.

2. If you have little or no success with #1, act as a mediator between the individuals.

3. Encourage listening and using "I" messages.

4. If there seems to be a deadlock with little progress, suggest time out for people to gather their thoughts and feelings.

5. Offer some informal training on conflict resolution.

6. Encourage win/win and compromise.

7. Set up an evaluation time to try out the suggested changes.

8. Encourage the expression of feelings between/among those involved.

9. Document! Cover Your Anatomy (C.Y.A.)!

10. Develop a conflict resolution policy for your program.

Sue's Solutions

What Really Works

If I'm going to be perfectly honest with you, and I am, this chapter is a good exercise for me. In fact, every time I teach a class on this topic, I learn something more about me and how I effectively I handle, or don't handle, conflict. I'm one of those people who would rather do flight than fight.

My parents didn't teach me the positive aspects of conflict. Whenever my mother and father disagreed, my father would go away in silence. My mother would slam things around. They didn't communicate to resolve the conflict.

So, I had to learn from wise people, other than my parents, how to deal positively with conflict and confrontation. Here are some tips I now use in my personal and professional lives:

6 Conflict is inevitable. If a relationship exists, some form of conflict exists. The people with whom we have the most contact, are the people with whom we have the most conflict.

6 Assertive behavior falls somewhere between that of a lap dog and a pit bull. At times you can choose to ignore conflict and decide to respond with "I don't care." When you do care, change your response, and let others know what you want or need. "I don't want you to go now." In handling conflicts, you want to stand somewhere in the middle of the two extremes of the Passive and Aggressive behavior the following words describe:

Passive	Aggressive
safe	pushy
cautious	bold
doormat	in-your-face
quiet	frustrated
introvert	demanding

Passive	Aggressive
reactive	controlling
not moving	goal-oriented
non-committal	dominant
· fear	my way

Do you get the picture? Assertive people know how to stand up for themselves without either backing down or running over the other person:

- They are decisive.

- They use direct eye contact.

- They are definite and specific.

- They aren't wishy-washy.

- They are not abrasive.

- They're clear and direct about what they want and need.

6   Good self-image is vital when handling a conflict situation. We need to feel self-assured and delete any negative self-talk that is going on inside of us. If someone is confronting you, it's okay to take a break and do some positive self-talk to keep your self-respect and pull yourself together. Seek out a coach who can objectively help you see your role in the situation. Then, go back and stand up for yourself.

6   Say this statement out loud, "Don't 'should' on yourself or others."

It sounds as though the statement has a double meaning, and it does. "Should" can be a judging and evaluating word. Your "shoulds" and my "shoulds" usually don't match, and they get in our way when dealing with conflict. Put yourself in the other person's shoes. Would you like to be on the receiving end of what you are saying?

6   Your beliefs are just thoughts. You have the power to change them. When you are in a conflict situation, remember to focus on the results, not on what's fair. Remember, too, that during

conflict, we need to remain flexible and promote win/win situations. Not all people in the conflict will walk away from it getting everything they want. Compromising and hearing what other people are saying are of key importance to conflict resolution. Again, our beliefs and belief systems are just thoughts, and we can change them.

6 Nonverbal communication or body language is 65% of communication—one strong argument for handling important confrontations in person. When you don't see the other person or persons, you can't read their body language.

6 People who get involved in conflict situations have varying beliefs about fight or flight. They either want to stay and fight or run away. The more people involved in the issue (such as staff or parents in your program), the more differing beliefs. Here are some of the beliefs that people have about conflict:

Positives	Negatives
1. Lots of things do work out.	1. Things never work out.
2. I don't need to argue to be powerful.	2. I feel helpless. Let's argue.
3. It's possible for everyone to win.	3. There are always winners and losers.
4. There are other ways.	4. This is just the way it is.
5. I am willing to be flexible.	5. I won't give up.

You can see by the above examples, people can enter into conflict with differing attitudes. A class participant gave me this reading about attitude—thoughts that I think all of us need to keep in mind when we are in a situation where we feel negative, cynical, or powerless:

Attitude

"The longer I live, the more I realize the impact of the attitude on life. Attitude, to me, is more important than facts. It is more important than the past, than education, than money, than circumstances, than failures, than successes, than what other people think or say or do. It is more important than appearance, giftedness, or skill. It will make or break a program . . . a church . . . a home . . . or a company. The remarkable thing is we have a choice every day regarding the attitude we will embrace for that day. We cannot change our past...we cannot change the fact that people will act in a certain way. We cannot change the inevitable. The only thing we can do is play on the one string we have, and that is our attitude . . . I am convinced that life is 10% what happens to me and 90% how I react to it. And so it is with you . . . we are in charge of our Attitudes." – Anonymous

6 Conflict within your program can be positive. Let's look at what can happen when we have constructive conflict or destructive conflict:

Constructive Conflict

- New ideas and perspectives surface.
- Evaluation of the organizational structure is possible.
- Discussion of upcoming decisions or problems takes place.
- The staff becomes energized and actively involved in the future of the program.

Destructive Conflict

- Staff members start taking sides with and against each other.
- Discussion never moves from complaints to solutions.
- Parents get drawn into the debate without full knowledge of the issue.
- Staff morale becomes affected because disagreements continue.
- Personalities of the staff become the focus rather than the initial issue of debate.

The staff needs to learn how to deal with conflict appropriately, without resorting to silence, apathy, and blaming; rather than looking for other options.

6 A simple conflict resolution script that you can teach your staff is:

When the children all run outside immediately after lunch,

The effect is that we are out of ratio; because we need two adults with them.

I feel angry because I am the one always stuck inside cleaning up.

I'd prefer to keep everyone inside until we can all go out together.

I appreciate your willingness to work with me on this issue.

You will note that no one is blaming or giving the other person reason to become defensive.

 6   In conflict situations, stay focused on: 1) what you want to have happen; 2) how you are feeling; 3) whether or not you're listening to the other person's response; and 4) obtaining a commitment from both parties to work on the issue.

 6   Listening is a necessary skill for resolving conflict. If you are unable (because you are responsible for ten children at the time) or unwilling (because you are too upset and feel defensive) to listen to the other person, let the person know that, rather than pretend to be listening. It's better to say, "I feel too distracted now to give you the attention this problem needs. Can we talk about it during nap time?"

 6   Decide if you want a *result* or if you *want to be right*. Be honest with your decision, because it will make a strong impact on how you handle the conflict.

 6   Fighting can be like dancing the tango. It takes two to do either. If you don't want to fight, move away from the other person.

 6   You **never** have to accept abuse during a confrontation or conflict situation. Abuse from anyone, directors, owners, or parents is unacceptable and destructive. Stop the discussion immediately and protect yourself from verbal, emotional, or physical abuse. Make sure that you, as a manager, also protect those you supervise.

Ask Yourself These Questions

How important is my self-esteem in conflict situations?
Very important. You will need to feel self-confident when you are
going to confront another person. Flood yourself with positive affirmations, and get support from others about your role in a conflict situation. Everything begins with a thought. Feelings and behaviors follow.

What do I want to have happen in conflict situations?
If we're going to take the time to address an issue with another person, most of us want to see results. It takes more energy to engage
negatively than it does to deal positively with another person. If we're
going to spend energy in a conflict situation, we want to see positive
results. We may not win everything we want, but compromising is
better than losing.

What will happen if the children see two adults arguing?
Conflict should be dealt with in private, but disagreements sometimes
happen in public. The adults in a child care program are role models for
children; children need to see that adults can disagree and still resolve
their issues. If the children see grown-ups handling conflict in non-con-
structive ways, they will learn negative ways to resolve differences.

**If I didn't have good role models when I was a child and I hate
to deal with conflict now as an adult, can I really change?**
Adults can change, if they want to. Don't remain a victim, living in
your past. As a responsible adult you can learn the skill of conflict resolution by reading books, taking classes, and practicing with a trusted
friend or relative.

Summary

I hope that, after reading this chapter, you have gained some new perspectives about how to handle little spats or huge disputes, remembering that conflict is inevitable. It's how we deal with it that matters.

All people you come in contact with have their own thoughts, feelings, and experiences about coping with conflict. You can't change the
other person's reactions to conflict, but you can change your own. You
can learn new and positive approaches that will minimize your level of
discomfort and offer a learning experience to others.

Personal Contract For Change

After reading the preceding chapter on how to resolve conflict, I'm ready to make the following changes:

Before reading this chapter, I approached conflict situations in the following manner:

    A.

    B.

    C.

Now that I have learned more about how I can handle conflict, I'm going to make these positive changes:

    A.

    B.

    C.

This is what I can do to create a climate in our program for healthy conflict:

    A.

    B.

    C.

These are techniques I can use for compromise and win-win situations during conflict:

    A.

    B.

    C.

_____   _____
       signed   date

I'm Too !+?Z= To Talk

THE MORE ANGRY WE ARE, THE WORSE OUR JUDGMENT IS.

Self Quiz

Anger can be very detrimental to personal well-being. Respond to the following statements about how anger affects you by checking yes or no after each statement, and totaling your score:

	YES	NO
1. I hesitate to, or I don't, express my angry feelings.	___	___
2. I don't express anger to people in authority.	___	___
3. I'm not satisfied with the way I handle other people's anger toward me.	___	___
4. I'm not satisfied with the way I handle my own feelings of anger.	___	___
5. I have felt angry for a long time.	___	___
6. My anger has caused disruptions at work or in relationships.	___	___
7. My body and emotions tell me when I'm feeling angry, but not dealing with it.	___	___
8. When I'm angry, I begin ranting and raving and using the word "You."	___	___
9. I experience more flight than fight responses.	___	___
10. I feel scared and defensive when other people get angry.	___	___
Total	___	___

Count how many yes responses you had. If you checked yes on five or more statements, now is the time that you start learning more about how you deal with your anger, as well as how anger affects your personal and professional lives. Don't get mad; just keep breathing and read on.

Survival Tips

Angry feelings occur in many situations, and when they do, we need to do something about them. You can use these survival tips in both your personal and professional lives:

1. Step back from the situation and take a deep breath.

2. Tell yourself that you don't have to take care of the situation immediately.

3. Find a non-biased person with whom you can vent. Ask that person for feedback and suggestions.

4. Try to see the situation from the other person's viewpoint.

5. Don't get into blaming, shaming, or name-calling.

6. When conflict with another individual is causing the anger, set aside a time to talk with that person.

7. Come up with three different ways you could handle a situation.

8. Pay attention to any physical symptoms you experience when you're angry.

9. Work out angry feelings with exercise.

10. Ask a parent or sibling to refresh your memory about how anger was dealt with when you were a child. This may help you understand how you deal with anger now.

11. Learn about dangers of stuffed anger—what it can do to you both physically and emotionally.

12. Consider seeking professional help if problems with anger persist.

Sue's Solutions

What Really Works

Anger is an emotion that really gets a bad rap. When children are angry they get sent to their rooms. People sometimes turn the powerful emotion of anger into rage and commit horrible acts of violence.

Anger is not bad. It's what we do with it that can be damaging. But we can learn from it, and that's what matters. Anger ranges from rage on the outside to hurt on the inside. Look at the following diagram; it illustrates some of the varying stages of anger:

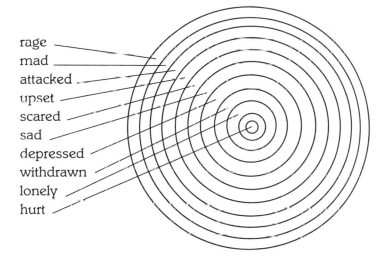

rage
mad
attacked
upset
scared
sad
depressed
withdrawn
lonely
hurt

The range of emotions goes from the outside layer, which is what other people see, to the inside of the circle, which only we feel, and which we share only with people we trust. This information is helpful to know about ourselves and others, because sometimes we see only the outside part and forget the many layers of emotion underneath.

When a parent comes in and starts yelling at you about her son being bitten by another toddler, you are seeing the anger on the outside; but the parent may be experiencing a lot of scared feelings inside. A technique called "active listening" can be useful when you want to let others know that you hear what they're saying.

Active listening is doing exactly what the phrase says: actively listening to the other person or other people. You may want to paraphrase what you are hearing them say. Ask clarifying questions, and ask for validation that what you hear them saying is correct. Warning: This technique will not work effectively for you if you are defensive; if you really don't want to take time to listen to the other person; or if you're trying to pay attention to your own anger. The following is an example of active listening:

Staff:	I am really angry about what happened in the staff meeting today.
Supervisor:	Can you say some more about that?
Staff:	It seemed like the preschool teachers were taking sides against our classroom.
Supervisor:	You felt they were picking on you?
Staff:	Yes, I guess I did.
Supervisor:	I can see how you might feel that way.

The conversation might go to a deeper level, or it might end with the staff person feeling that you heard his or her concerns. The next time you feel angry at someone, remember these points:

6 EXIT OR WAIT. Allow some cooling down time so you don't say or do something that you might regret.

6 USE THE WORD "I" NOT "YOU." Own what you're saying and feeling rather than blaming the other person for your feelings.

6 STAY IN THE PRESENT. Don't dig up past wounds or project into the future about what might happen. Stick to what you're feeling now.

6 FOCUS ON THE ESSENTIAL. What is it that you're really angry about? Learn how to choose your battles.

6 AVOID PHYSICAL FORCE AND THREATS. It's never permissible to become physical with another person when you're angry.

Don't make threats; they only accelerate the other person's anger. Think before you speak or act.

⑥ KEEP IT SHORT AND TO THE POINT. When people are at the height of anger, only a few words get heard. Be brief and direct about what you want to say. You can go into more detail after a cooling down period.

⑥ PUT IT IN WRITING. You can write down what you want to say to the other person or persons and either give it to them or destroy it, and use the exercise as a form of purging your feelings.

⑥ RESTORE GOOD FEELINGS. If you care about a future relationship, whether with an individual or a group of people, take time to express how you value them.

⑥ Dealing with anger involves taking a careful look at ourselves and understanding our style of handling anger. Here are four ways of doing that:

1) STUFFING–moving away from directly confronting the person or situation that's provoking the anger. Stuffing reflects a flight response and is not effective because–

- the anger comes out sideways at the wrong person;
- you may kick the dog;
- the ongoing provocation continues;
- unaddressed anger can cause personal health problems.

2) BLAMING–refusing to take responsibility for your own feelings and blaming others.

3) ESCALATING–begins usually with starting sentences with the word "you." Ranting and raving are characteristic of this style, which doesn't work; because constant and intense anger makes others more angry.

Escalating anger also physically damages your own body. Violence can enter into a relationship when this style occurs. You may get your way, but only in the short run; because this style of dealing with anger does nothing to enhance a relationship.

4) DIRECTING—expressing your feelings directly to the provoking person. You say what you are feeling and thinking without using any of the previously mentioned techniques. You can express anger in a positive manner, and directing your anger is the productive way to handle it.

Did you see yourself in one of these anger styles? Awareness is the first step to creating changes in our lives. Some anger can do a great deal of internal damage. Have you ever heard someone say that they never saw their parents fight or have an argument, but that their father died at an early age from a heart attack?

It's true that people who let anger eat at their insides are more prone to physical ailments. If you start having physical symptoms such as ulcers, headaches, depression, or chemical abuse, please pay attention to the warning signs; and make immediate changes on how you manage your anger.

Ask Yourself These Questions

Everyone has angry feelings. They're normal. We need to look at what we do about them. Ask yourself the following questions about your thoughts and feelings around anger:

When I was little, how was anger addressed in my family?
The way we saw anger addressed when we were children has great impact on what we do with this emotion when we become adults. Many people still deal with anger as they did when they were little kids. They pout, blame other people for their feelings, cry, throw things around, say things they really don't mean, and slam doors when they run away. Sound familiar?

When my father used silence as his way of coping with anger, he would retreat from the situation and would not talk to anyone for a long time. As a child, this scared me because I never knew who or what he was mad about; and I also didn't know if he would return. As an adult, I am learning different and more healthy ways to take care of my anger.

Do I know specific cues that trigger my anger?

These triggers can also be referred to as "pushing your buttons."
When people start "shoulding" on me, I can feel myself become
defensive. When people either become silent, like my father, or start
banging things around without provocation, like my mother, it takes
me right back to being a little kid again. Such personal life experiences trigger people's emotions.

Some people become overly sensitive and irate, for example,
whenever they're lied to; because they were lied to in an important
relationship. Learn what your own, personal triggers are; and pay
attention to them when you feel yourself becoming angry.

Do I use flight or fight when I become angry?

Do you go away when you become angry, or do you strike out? A
cooling down period is very appropriate when one becomes angry.
The time also allows us to possibly vent with someone else before
we come back to the other person. Cooling down is different from
stuffing anger or abandoning those who make us angry.

Cooling down is a technique for the short term. After we cool
down we manage the situation in a productive way. Remember that
the children and other staff in your program are watching you. They
see you as a role model, and you can teach them that it's okay to
feel angry and to take care of those feelings without hurting someone else.

What am I afraid will happen when I become angry?

Knowing you have fears about what will happen when you're angry
is important information to have about yourself, and about others
with whom you have a relationship. Some people are afraid of losing control, having the other person mad at them, hurting someone
else's feelings, or having people leave them.

If you know what scares you, and you can recognize it, you can
address your feelings appropriately. The information you have about
other people is not to be used to hurt them, but to help them when
they are going through their fears and anger. The more knowledge
you have about the emotions of fear and anger and how they inter-
act, the better you will be at managing professional and personal
relationships.

Summary

Fortunately, times are changing. We are learning and teaching others that anger isn't a negative emotion, but a feeling that happens within all of us. It can be a most powerful emotion, but one that we can turn into a positive tool to motivate us to resolve stressful situations. It's okay for all of us to feel anger, but it's not okay to let the feelings build up inside like spinach in a pressure cooker.

I hope this chapter helped you learn something about yourself and the people you work with, about how you handle anger, but especially how to release the steam slowly so the spinach (anger) doesn't explode all over you and everyone else.

Personal Contract For Change

After reading the preceding chapter on anger, I'm going to make the following changes in my personal and professional lives:

When I feel myself becoming angry, I'm going to tell myself:

    A.

    B

    C.

These are the changes I'm going to make in my negative behaviors around anger:

    A.

    B.

    C.

When I feel myself becoming defensive, I'm going to:

    A.

    B.

    C.

I'm going to take these steps to address my angry feelings with others on both a personal and professional level:

    A.

    B.

    C.

_____   _____
       signed   date

Delegating is More Than Just Dumping

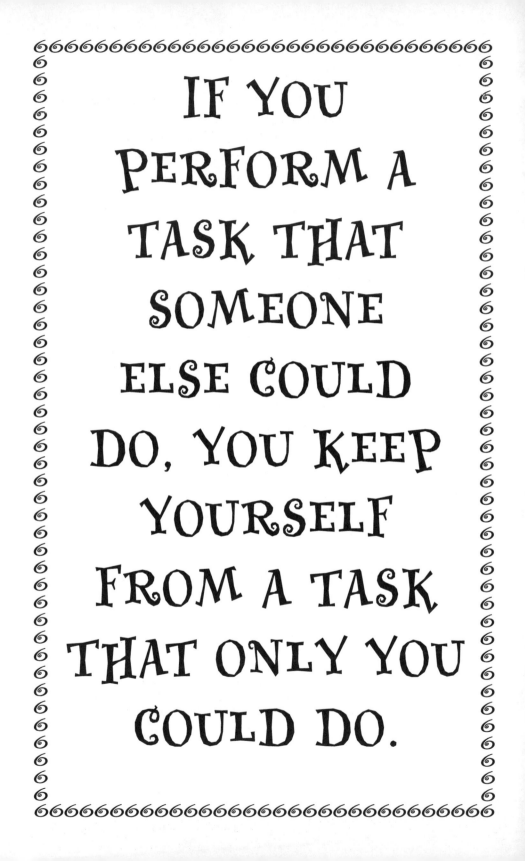

IF YOU PERFORM A TASK THAT SOMEONE ELSE COULD DO, YOU KEEP YOURSELF FROM A TASK THAT ONLY YOU COULD DO.

Self Quiz

Delegating is a survival tool that enhances the experience and self-esteem of other people and decreases some of your more time-consuming tasks as a supervisor. This self quiz will help you determine if you need to further develop your delegating skills. Check yes or no as honestly as you can:

	YES	NO
1. It's easier and quicker to do things myself.	___	___
2. The staff won't like me if I expect too much of them.	___	___
3. I can do most of the supervisory work better than anyone else.	___	___
4. I'm not sure to whom I should delegate.	___	___
5. Our program is usually understaffed and I have no one to whom I can delegate.	___	___
6. I have a hard time asking others to do things for me.	___	___
7. I'm afraid the staff will think I'm dumping my job on them.	___	___
8. If mistakes occur with something I delegate, I correct them myself.	___	___
9. I think I might have a problem with trying to control too much.	___	___
10. I am afraid my staff will resent my requests for help.	___	___
Total	___	___

If you checked yes on three or more of the above statements, continue reading this chapter. If you checked yes on all of the above statements, speed read this chapter; and start getting some help from others immediately.

Survival Tips

1. Recognize that you are human, that you can't do everything yourself.

2. Create a balance between too little and too much followup for each project.

3. Let go of non-management tasks that someone else could do, e.g.: attendance forms, grocery shopping, and paper work.

4. Recognize employee accomplishments with praise and statements of appreciation.

5. Give credit where and to whom credit is due.

6. Don't overburden your best and most trusted staff because you have not prepared anyone else.

7. Let the staff know in advance about tasks you'll be delegating with personal notes or with notations in the program log book.

8. Teach staff members to solve their own problems to help prepare them for delegation.

9. When staff is in a decision-making process, let the process continue without your involvement.

10. Remember that delegating is one way to use and reinforce creative talents.

11. Make a list of staff skills and possible tasks they can do.

12. Delegate the authority that goes along with the task.

13. Enjoy working less than an 80-hour work week.

14. Let parents know about the new projects staff are doing through the newsletter, or in conversation.

Sue's Solutions

What Really Works

Have you ever listened to people complain about too much to do and too little time? Trying to help, you offer them advice about how to give some of their work to other people. They reply "Oh! I can't. Others can't do it as well as I can." Delegating is a skill that enables you to let go of tasks others could do so you will have time to do what takes your expertise. Often, I ask staff how they feel when they have a task delegated to them. They reply, "I feel that the manager trusts me to take care of an important issue with a parent," or "It makes me feel good to know that I am asked to help out with something that needs my special skills."

We assume that others will think that our requests are an extra burden, but we don't check it out with them first.

Two forms of delegation are:

Formal delegation: a task that is placed in an employee's job description and is included in the employee's performance evaluation.

Informal delegation: a verbal or written request that may occur one or more times. An informal delegation that is ongoing could become a formal one.

Delegation should not only benefit the asker, but also the doer. The person asking for help gets the needed assistance. The person helping out learns new skills, gets professional recognition, and becomes more valuable to the program.

6   When I do everything myself, I feel very much in control. I also feel angry, overwhelmed, and exhausted; but I do feel in control. Ask yourself what the control is costing you. Do you share some of my feelings?

6   When I was a director, we had to have groceries for our program. I assumed the role of Chief Grocery Shopper. I thought I could get the best deals for the money and do the job faster

than anyone else in the program. Then came the long winter months. I delegated the grocery shopping to a parent who was willing to do the job for a reduction in tuition. She benefited from taking on this responsibility, and I saved wear and tear on both my car and my body. And guess what? The grocery bill went down.

6   Although we believe we can do everything faster and better than anyone else in the program, delegating can save money. Ask yourself if it's costing more money to have the director or supervisor do tasks, like grocery shopping, than it would cost to delegate the chore to someone else. Others can do these jobs, allowing you more time for tasks only you can do.

Let's look at some of the roadblocks to delegation and possible solutions to these barriers:

Roadblock	Solution
1. If the other person doesn't do it right, I'll look bad.	1. Delegate to those who you know have the ability to complete the task.
2. The task could be done by someone else, but it would take longer to delegate than to do the job myself.	2. Have someone start to learn the process. They will soon be able to do the task on a regular basis.
3. I can delegate only meaningless busy work.	3. This technique creates resentments. Give the staff some of the tasks you like to do, but could give up.
4. The staff resists the work, saying that they don't know how to do it.	4. Break down the job and let staff handle as many components as they can. Add more when they are ready. Provide training.

Roadblock	Solution
5. If the staff can do a lot of the extra jobs, then maybe I won't be needed.	5. Supervisors are always needed to deal with the fine tuning of the program. Keep doing tasks that require your specialized abilities.
6. When I delegate a task, the staff keeps coming back for advice and help.	6. Whenever staff asks how you would do the task, turn the question around and ask them how they would do it. Reinforce correct answers without becoming angry. Help them build confidence.
7. Staff might not meet the deadlines.	7. Clearly state the deadline and let the staff know why it must be met. Identify reasons for missing deadlines and take corrective action.
8. Staff might not do things the way I do them.	8. Focus on getting the right results and learn to live with the differences. Their way of doing something might even be better than your way.
9. Their performance might jeopardize a successful outcome	9. Identify reasons they might not be successful and take corrective action. You might have to change the level of authority and provide more support.

What Can I Delegate?

Here's a list of specific tasks that directors, program managers, and supervisors report delegating to other staff:

1. Planning the lists for supplies, program materials, and groceries.

2. Shopping for all of the above.

3. Scheduling substitutes (Don't throw your hands up in the air quite yet. It can be done.) The director's job is to develop and maintain the substitute list, but the designated staff person can receive the phone calls requesting the need for a sub, schedule the substitute, and then, make sure the director is advised.

4. Planning and bringing treats to the staff meeting.

5. Setting up parent conferences.

6. Performing specific tasks for a special event.

7 Setting up weekly curriculum for the classroom.

8. Doing bulletin boards.

9. Keeping daily records for the classroom.

10. Proofreading policies for parents, the program, and the staff.

11. Cleaning the infamous store room every program has.

12. Contributing to the program newsletter.

13. Leading a workshop or a staff meeting.

14. Making a supply list for each classroom.

If you are having trouble delegating, start off slowly; and pick tasks to delegate that seem easy, simple, and non-threatening. Tell someone you trust that you're trying to work on delegating, and ask for help with your decisions.

Ask Yourself These Questions

What's stopping me?
Begin by figuring out why you don't delegate. Some possibilities include: inability to give up control; lack of confidence in staff; fear of possible repercussions; perfectionism; importance of the task to be delegated; discomfort with staff perceptions; unwillingness to impose on people; insufficient time to organize the project; and difficulty explaining the task to others. Recognize and remove all roadblocks.

Who benefits from my delegating?
Delegating benefits everyone. You get the assistance you need. The staff members learn new skills, become more valuable to the program, and get professional recognition. The parents could be eligible to receive tuition reimbursement for repairing equipment or fixing up the building. Even the children benefit when you show them other staff are capable of performing managerial duties such as making plans for the upcoming field trip.

How do I decide what to give up?
When your body is sending you strong messages (head pounding, stomach in a knot, or other stress-related physical symptoms) about some of the upcoming tasks that must be completed, ask yourself if staff could do the pending jobs as well as you can. This is the time to practice what you've learned in this chapter. The key factor to remember is that delegating empowers others to take on new responsibilities while freeing you for the tasks that only you can do.

Summary

Delegating is a skill that takes both practice and determination to make it work. Some of the staff may resist when you begin to delegate. If you find yourself becoming discouraged, talk with a peer to see if your requests seem reasonable. Use assertive techniques that include keeping your requests simple and stating them in a direct and straightforward manner. Your attitude is important when you are making requests of other people. You have a right to make these requests. Keep in mind that you're not dumping on others, you are enabling them to become more responsible and educated in a particular skill.

Personal Contract For Change

After reading this chapter, I am going to assess my ability to delegate.

I realize that I have the following fears about delegating to others:

A. _____

B. _____

C. _____

D. _____

E. _____

I'm going to delegate the following tasks to the following people and allow them to be responsible for the outcome:

	Task	Person	By When
A.	_____	_____	_____
B.	_____	_____	_____
C.	_____	_____	_____
D.	_____	_____	_____

I'm going to turn my negative messages about delegating into positive affirmations:

	Negative Message		Positive Affirmation
A.	_____	A.	_____
B.	_____	B.	_____
C.	_____	C.	_____

_____   _____
         signed   date

Risk-Taking
For Managers

EVERYTHING A PERSON WANTS IN LIFE INVOLVES TAKING A RISK.

Self Quiz

There is simply no way to grow without taking chances. This self quiz will give you the opportunity to test your comfort level with risk-taking. Check yes or no after each statement. Then, total your score and read this chapter for further tips.

	YES	NO
1. I become anxious just thinking about taking risks.	___	___
2. I was raised with the philosophy of "better safe than sorry."	___	___
3. Sometimes I have a hard time making decisions for fear that my decision will be wrong.	___	___
4. I have had regrets about not taking certain chances in my life.	___	___
5. The fear of getting hurt stops me from taking a risk.	___	___
6. I want to be sure that events will turn out the way I expect.	___	___
7. I have a hard time deciding if I will lose or gain by risking.	___	___
8. I'm afraid of people rejecting either me or my ideas.	___	___
9. Sometimes I think of risk-taking as all or nothing.	___	___
10. In the past, I have been stuck in the fear of change and unable to take any action to move forward.	___	___
Total	___	___

If you checked yes on three or more statements, this chapter with its tips on taking risks, is for you Remember, you are in charge of your life and will decide when and how to make changes.

Survival Tips

1. Begin the process of risk-taking with small steps.

2. Stay away from all-or-nothing decisions.

3. You can decide to not make a decision, which is also a decision.

4. Ask yourself "If I do this, what is the worst thing that will happen?"

5. Solicit support from trusted friends and colleagues to help you take more risks.

6. Choose safety over risking when it comes to the care of children.

7. Observe others who are more adept at taking risks than you are, and evaluate their gains and losses.

8. Learn how to evaluate your progress when it comes to change and risk.

9. Don't let regrets keep you from taking risks. Know that you have the right to change your mind at any time.

10. Ask yourself how the issues of control and power play a part in your willingness to take risks.

11. If you were raised with the philosophy of "better safe than sorry," decide if this is getting in the way of your growth and progress.

12. Give yourself and others permission to make mistakes.

13. Try something new that will give you personal feelings of success for having discovered new possibilities within yourself.

14. Discover a new skill that will help you feel better about yourself.

Sue's Solutions

What Really Works

I have two daughters who are totally opposite when it comes to taking risks. My younger daughter, Carrie, believes that life itself is a risk and should be lived to its fullest. I attribute many of my gray hairs to her philosophy. Fortunately for me, she has made a point of waiting until after the event to tell me about the risks she's taken. My older daughter, Kris, is much more cautious and reserved. She will take more time to make decisions, putting safety ahead of risk-taking. I could see the differences in their individual risk-taking styles when they were toddlers.

I'm a combination of both my daughters. I'm usually rather cautious about taking risks, but when I decided to leave my thirteen-year position with the Early Childhood Directors Association, I made my decision quickly. That was one of the most risky decisions I have ever made. I left a job that provided me with a regular pay check, benefits, and security. I started my own training and consulting company which provided me with none of the above. I definitely took a leap of faith toward something unknown, and three years later I can say that it was the right decision.

Let's look at some specific tips that work for moving out of the better-safe-than-sorry mode to nothing ventured, nothing gained.

6 What words would you use to describe yourself?

___careful	___overly cautious
___safe	___risky
___adventurous	___fearful
___decisive	___guarded

Do you are see a pattern that fits you? We can blend our personal and professional risk-taking styles. However, when we are responsible for the lives of others, we may tend to be more willing to take chances in our personal lives than in our professional lives. Managers who work in child care know they must remain cautious about some things. Safety is vital and essential for all the children in your program.

6   The first step in risk-taking is to make a decision. You will experience times in your program when you can't afford to be wishy-washy, times when being firmly decisive is important, when the children, other staff, and parents will look to you to be the decision maker. If this is a problem for you, keep reading.

6   Fear is often a factor that gets in the way of taking risks. Can you identify with any of the following fears?
The fear of:

failure

competition

disapproval

confrontation

being wrong

change

intimacy

rejection

success

Many changes can appear to be threatening and unsettling: a new position, someone on staff getting fired or promoted, the end of a relationship or a career change. Try to think of changes as opportunities that will allow you to have new experiences from which to personally grow and develop.

6   Many of us are terrified at the possibility of loss; and therefore, we try to avoid risking at all costs. Not risking is the surest way of losing. If a new position is posted in your program, and you're thinking about applying, but you're afraid of being rejected, your hesitancy might cost you the job. If you apply and get offered the position, you can decide then if the job is something that is really right for you. "She Who Snoozes, Loses" is a saying to remember when we're considering waiting to make up our minds.

6 Before you decide to take a risk, understand and evaluate these decision-making processes. You could:

- Decide to make the decision yourself without consulting others.

- Collaborate with others and consider their thoughts on the subject.

- Bargain with another person so that, if you lose, your loss will be less than if you take the risk alone.

6 As you decide to take a risk, consider the following four tips:

- Personal growth requires that you loosen your control on what you already can do and move beyond your comfort zone into the unknown. Sometimes this can feel like walking into a dark room.

- Start small and build self-confidence. Take risks only when you can handle the loss. If the risk would be detrimental or catastrophic to you or others, don't take it in its present form.

- Get more information about the pending risk. You will improve the odds for success and reduce the chances of loss. Ask questions, take more time, or involve others whom you trust in your decision-making process.

- Know that sometimes you might fail. Allow yourself to make mistakes and learn from those you make. Consider mistakes you and others make as an opportunity for growth.

6 Evaluating who your decision would affect is important. If you're deciding about changing careers, you may be the only one affected. However, if you're making a decision about expanding your program, you will have many factors to consider; and your decision-making process will be very different.

6 You're a role model for others when it comes to making decisions and taking risks. If you work with other staff who are having difficulty in this area, you can train them by your example. Child care professionals are in positions where they make hundreds of decisions daily. You don't want to encourage them to take unnecessary risks when it comes to the safety and well-being of the children.

Ask Yourself These Questions

How can I make the reward and loss ratio more balanced when I make decisions?

Sometimes you can share the risk with others. You can ask others to give you input into the decision-making process. Although they're not responsible for the outcome, they can offer you support. You can also decide what an unacceptable loss would be, and make your decision on that information. For example, if you were deciding about taking the toddlers on a field trip, you could ask for other opinions. But if the weather looks ominous, you could decide not to take the field trip based on what might happen with severe weather conditions. The safety of the children is the important factor in this decision.

How much time should I spend gathering information from others about a decision that I have to make?

It depends on the importance of the decision and who will gain or suffer from your actions. Deciding when to do a staff retreat may necessitate getting availability information from other staff, and then, taking action. Terminating a staff member may require substantiating your decision before putting your actions into place.

I have taken risks that were dangerous and impulsive. How can I weave caution into my plan of action?

Slow down, and think before you act. Consult with others about their opinions and viewpoints before making final decisions. Consider how your decisions will affect others.

Summary

I have addressed two different philosophies of risk-taking and change: "better safe than sorry" and "nothing ventured, nothing gained." It's important for child care professionals, or any other professionals who care for other people, to use moderation when developing a personal philosophy on risk and change.

When I used to think of taking risks, I would see myself bouncing on a high diving board, waiting to go into thirteen feet of water below. Often, I would freeze there and just keep bouncing on the board without jumping in. Then, I changed the picture in my mind. I now think of risk-taking as standing on the edge of a lake with the soft waves coming in. I can wade out and get my feet wet and go back to the shore when I think I need to. As I gain more confidence, I will wade farther out.

Practice taking small risks, and as your self-esteem and confidence improves, wade farther out and take larger risks. As your self-awareness increases you will be able to see a clearer picture of the rewards of your risk-taking.

Personal Contract For Change

After reading the chapter on risk-taking, I want to make the following changes:

These are some risks I want to take:

     A.

     B.

     C.

These are some of the fears I want to overcome:

     A.

     B.

     C.

These are resources I have to help me with my fears:

     A.

     B.

     C.

These are commitments I've been avoiding:

     A.

     B.

     C.

These are commitments I'm going to make to myself and others:

     A.

     B.

     C.

_____   _____

       signed   date

Where Do I Go
From Here?

OUR VALUES AFFIRM THE PURPOSE AND MEANING OF OUR WORK.

Self Quiz

Questioning our career choices is normal. We do that from time to time, and sometimes we feel we may need a change; but we're not sure that a career move is the answer. This self quiz will help you determine if you're at the point of needing to make internal or external shifts in your job as a child care manager. Check yes or no after the following statements and then total your score.

	YES	NO
1. I'm feeling discontent and unhappy in my present job.	___	___
2. I don't see the stress that I am experiencing as being time-limited.	___	___
3. I have recently been looking in the classified section of the paper for other job openings.	___	___
4. Lately I have been less tolerant with people at work.	___	___
5. I enjoy working with the children but have a more difficult time with the adults.	___	___
6. My self-esteem has lessened at work, and I have more self-doubts.	___	___
7. I've been talking with others about the concerns I have with my job.	___	___
8. The current problems within our program don't seem to be within my control.	___	___
9. I'm not sure if the changes that are needed are within me or with the program.	___	___
10. I think I have outgrown my current position.	___	___
Total	___	___

If you checked yes on three or more of the above statements, you might want to do more self-exploration about your values and personal self-worth. Read this chapter before you make any hasty decisions.

Survival Tips

1. Recognize and accept that any managerial position in child care will have a certain amount of stress.

2. Check your personal and professional attitude. Is it your attitude or the job that needs the adjustment?

3. Take a personal retreat for the necessary time you need to do an internal check of your values, career, and life goals.

4. Research the topic of career and life planning either through books or through classes you can take in a community education program or at a local college.

5. Talk to trusted colleagues who are familiar with your work situation. Ask for their input as to whether the problems you're experiencing are within you or in your program.

6. Decide if what you are setting out to do in life is getting swept away by the needs of others.

7. Place an importance on how you lead your life. Your values, vision, goals, and conscience should direct your future.

8. Check the balance in your life. If your life is out of balance for one reason or another, it will be more difficult to make a rational decision about your future. Working 60 hours a week does not allow much time for inner-soul searching.

9. Evaluate your position in your child care program. Is there room for professional growth within the organization? Are you interested in changing your position?

10. Relax in a hammock or in a bubble bath and fantasize about your ideal job.

11. One morning on your way to work, visualize yourself driving to another job. Where would it be and what would you be doing?

12. Make a list of the pros and cons of your current job. Pay attention to the length of each of the lists.

13. Decide if this job fits your natural abilities. Would you rather be leading a staff meeting with adults or leading a group time with children?

14. As I tell children in swimming classes, "Keep breathing!" It will help keep you afloat while you assess your future.

Sue's Solutions

What Really Works

In the previous chapter on risk-taking I said that three years ago I left my administrative position. Although this decision may have seemed abrupt to some of my peers, others who knew me well were not surprised. I believe that our personal values must match our professional work, and if they are not in unison, it may be time for a change.

I knew I needed to do the consulting and training work that I think makes a difference in people's lives. I wanted to write a book to support managers. I wanted to work for myself.

Changes may take place within our jobs, and we may then decide to stay, or we may choose to find another position. I chose to follow a new direction that seemed right for me.

Here are some tips that will help you decide on changes you may want to make:

6 Evaluating your current personal and professional lives is quite an intense process. You should be in a mind set that allows you to be objective. If your self-esteem seems to be faltering or you are in some kind of crisis, recognize that you need to deal with these issues before you can be objective.

6 The issue of age plays a factor in career and life planning. The process of development begins in childhood and continues throughout adulthood. Stating an age at which each stage occurs is difficult, because just as children do, adults go through developmental stages at varying ages.

The following are Erikson's Adult Stages:	
• Identity:	Who am I?
• Intimacy:	Can I be committed and close to others?
• Generativity:	Can I nurture others?
• Ego Integrity:	Am I satisfied with my life?

Some of us go through the different stages faster than others. Some of us get stuck in certain stages. Can you find the stage that you are currently in? Can you identify the stage that your colleagues at work seem to be in? Learning to appreciate differences is important in this area. You may be in the Ego Integrity stage; and because the other staff you work with are much younger than you are, they're in the Identifying stage. As you go through your career and life-planning search, don't compare yourself to others. Focus on what's right for you.

6 Dedicated child care managers are committed to working in the field of early childhood, but they sometimes need a change from their current positions. Here are examples of people who left managerial positions to take other jobs within the child care field:

- Teacher a' a technical college for students who want to work in the child care field.

- Field representative for a local early childhood supply company.

- Classroom teacher in another program working only with children and not supervising other adults.

- Training coordinator for a child care agency.

- Counselor for a Resource and Referral agency.

- Family Child Care Provider

- Director of a child care advocacy program.

- Owner of a preschool program.

- Editor and acquisitions specialist for an early childhood publishing company.

- Owner and operator of a child care substitute service.

- Curriculum coordinator for a group of child care programs.

- Field representative for a child and adult care food program.

- Facilities manager for a retreat center.

6   Another choice we have in this decision-making process is to continue in our current positions with some changes. Here are some of the changes that managers made within their personal and professional lives, without changing their positions:

- Went back to school to take classes in business and administration management. These managers were able to use this information in their current positions as managers, and to develop new skills in case they decide to change jobs.

- Reduced their positions to half or three-quarter time, allowing the option for a different part-time job without burning out by working two full-time positions. Sometimes the new job was in child care; at other times it was in an unrelated field.

- Worked in a part-time teaching position at a local technical college. The new role offered the opportunity to work with students in the child care field; and as managers, to recruit additional part-time substitutes.

Trying changes such as these might provide you with the time you need to decide if leaving your current job is the right decision. You might not be able to make all the necessary changes for an ideal job, but changing something in the picture may open up areas that you had not thought of before.

Ask Yourself These Questions

How will I know that I need a change?
Three reasons not to stay in your current job:

1. You can no longer tolerate the current situation, for whatever reasons.

2. Your dissatisfaction is causing significant problems in your performance, which could put you or others you work with at risk.

3. Your unhappiness is ruining the rest of your life.

If even one of the three above statements fits you now, take action and decide if you or the job need to change.

How quickly should I move through this process of career and life exploration?

Life's not a race. As we tell parents, life is a process; and the process is what we focus on, more than the final product. Pay attention to what's within yourself, and begin the process of internal exploration before you are in a crisis situation.

What are some key factors I can use to decide if I have outgrown my current position?

The majority of child care managers have come through the ranks in early childhood. Most are trained to work with children, but fall into the position of supervising other adults. Due to the lack of supervisory training, many become frustrated and impatient with themselves and others.

Ask yourself the following questions to determine if you are outgrowing your current position:

- Am I bored with my job?

- Am I feeling unchallenged with my current job duties?

- Am I frustrated with the level of competence of other staff?

- Am I feeling stuck and discontent?

- Am I feeling overwhelmed with personal and professional issues in my life?

If you answered yes to any of the above questions, become proactive with your career and life-exploration process. No matter what stage of development you are currently in, it never hurts to evaluate where you've been, where you are now, and what lies ahead.

Summary

We've all heard the phrase, "Life is not a dress rehearsal," which is appropriate to any discussion of life exploration. The internal growth process begins with birth and continues until we die.

Knowing that we continually have the power of choice makes life interesting, just as feeling stuck can be detrimental to both our personal and professional lives. Becoming proactive in our exploration of career and life planning is the key to success. When we make decisions and move forward, we may flounder, but rarely do we drown. People are there to help coach us, and paying attention to others and ourselves is what life is all about.

Take the tips that are in this chapter. Apply them to your daily living. When it comes to making decisions about your career, don't wait for others to act on your behalf. Take action and decide how you want to spend the days, weeks, and years of your life.

Personal Contract For Change

After reading this, I am going to examine where I go from here in the following ways:

I will seek out these colleagues who can objectively help me assess my current professional status:

      A.

      B.

      C.

I will use these problems and possible solutions in my decision-making process:

Problems	Solutions
A.	A.
B.	B.
C.	C.

I will look at these as other directions I could pursue if I were to decide to change careers:

      A.

      B.

      C.

I will recognize these starts and stops that will affect my ability to make a decision about my future:

What Works	What Gets In My Way
A.	A.
B.	B.
C.	C.

_____   _____

        signed   date